VIETNAM NORTH

VIETNAM
NORTH

by Wilfred G. Burchett

INTERNATIONAL PUBLISHERS

New York

Library of Congress Catalog Card Number: 66–28970
Manufactured in the United States of America

CONTENTS

ILLUSTRATIONS

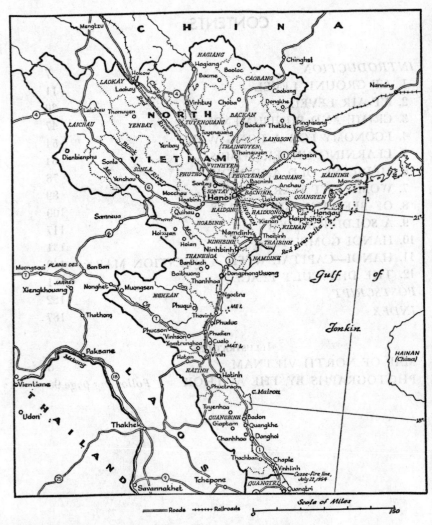

© 1966 by The New York Times Company. Reprinted by permission.

INTRODUCTION

"Prepare for the worst" was a phrase I was to hear often during two visits to North Vietnam in February and April–May, 1966. It has almost become a national slogan, certainly among those who direct the country's military and economic strategy. The government of the North, the Democratic Republic of Vietnam (DRV), is organizing in a manner without precedent in history for the long, hard war which leaders and people are convinced will have to be fought.

Almost every day of the seven weeks I spent in the DRV brought its surprises.

A forest clearing led down to a limpid stream, where rafts of bamboo, attached to the bank with jungle creepers, stretched up-stream like corrugated footpaths. Lines of young people jog-trotted along, up the river bank toward the clearing, 50-foot-lengths of giant bamboo swinging between their shoulders. In the clearing itself, more youths and girls sawed sectioned tree trunks into thin planks and pleated leaves for roofs. Further back in the jungle shadows, in new bamboo and pleated-leaf buildings, young people, visible through the propped-up bamboo "windows"—which were also the walls—bent over desks and books.

"This is C5," explained my guide, "the metallurgical section of the Polytechnic Institute. On the very day the main new building of the Institute was opened in Hanoi, C5 opened its course here for the first quarter of the 1965–66 scholastic year. Most other faculties are also evacuated."

"Isn't it an awful waste?" I asked one of the French-speaking professors. "Hanoi hasn't been bombed. The Americans even say they don't intend to bomb Hanoi."

"We can't rely on what those bandits say," he replied. "We must prepare for the worst. The government attaches great importance to protecting our students, the future technical cadres."

How right was the professor, and Hanoi's leaders who had

encouraged this realistic attitude, was proven a couple of months later when American planes bombed the fuel depots in Hanoi's outskirts and those at Haiphong on the fringe of the most densely populated area of that city.

"Prepare for the worst," however, was more than a slogan. It was the expression of a concrete, organizational revolution in the country's life—and of a sober analysis of American intentions.

"Let Johnson and his clique well understand," said President Ho Chi Minh in his appeal to world opinion on July 17, 1966, "they can send 500,000 troops, a million or even more to intensify the war of aggression in South Vietnam. They can use thousands of planes to intensify their attacks against the North. But they will never break the iron will of the heroic Vietnamese people to fight against American aggression, for national salvation. . . . There is nothing more precious than independence and liberty."

"Prepare for the worst" went on in every field of activity and at every level as the 17 million people of the North rolled up their sleeves, stripped themselves to the waist and prepared, literally with bare hands in many cases, to take on the world's greatest military and industrial power, in what must be one of the most cruelly unequal confrontations in world history. I had glimpses of how this process was shaping up every day, almost every hour of my visit.

Rolling along a road in the coastal areas, admiring a field of six-inch-high maize, I suddenly saw the "field" scramble to its feet, peasant men and women, their backs swathed in green leaves, rifles and light machine guns in hand rushing to roadside defensive positions. I had to look back at the field to make sure that there really was a young maize crop there. "Maneuvers of the local self-defense corps in case the Americans make landings in the area," my guide explained.

"But surely you don't expect the Americans to land in the North?"

"They'll be mad if they do but our defenses are based on this possibility. We have to prepare for the worst."

In a beautiful centuries-old Buddhist pagoda, carved roof dragons silhouetted against a golden sky as the sun dropped down, scores of lacquered Buddhas gazed benignly down on patients from an evacuated Hanoi district hospital, laid out in camp beds between the altars. A white-gowned nurse pedalled with her hands an upturned bicycle, wires leading from the ordinary cycle-lamp dynamo into a small cabin, isolated by mosquito netting. On the other end of the wires and inside the cabin, under the feeble light of a six-volt lamp, a surgeon and nurses bent over a patient, for a stomach operation.

"But there are electric power lines only a kilometer away," I protested. "In a matter of hours you could have light and power laid in."

"True," said the Public Health Ministry official with me, "but our surgeons and medical teams must prepare for the worst. They must get used to operating under emergency conditions. If the escalation continues, we cannot always count on having electric light and power around."

A famous old grotto with a hundred yards or so of rock above it was inhabited by bats and a few stone statues when I last visited it. Now there was the steady hum of machinery. Galleries which led off in all directions from the mouth of the main grotto had been widened and reinforced, generators installed in some; lathes, jigs, borers, grinders and polishers and other machines in others—an entire vital industrial unit in full production.

The caves, mountains, forests and villages of North Vietnam are the repository of secrets and sources of strength until recently concentrated in Hanoi and other cities. It is on this sort of material and psychological redeployment of forces that the Hanoi leaders base their faith in victory, not on MIG's or missiles or other gadgetry of modern war. They acknowledge that the latter also have their place, but not a decisive one.

How does an underdeveloped country of 17 million, with an overwhelmingly agricultural economy envisage waging—and winning—a war against the richest, most highly industrialized, most militarily powerful country in the world? Why the confident smiles on the faces of Ho Chi Minh, Pham Van Dong, Vo Nguyen Giap and the others? It was the answer to such questions, and to such smiles, that I sought during my visit to the North.

In talks with the country's top political and military leaders, with the heads of the various ministries directing the country's economic, social and cultural reorganization; in visits to the new construction sites and evacuated industries; to the zones where bombings had reached saturation point—traveling often over bridges the Americans claimed destroyed, along roads they claimed had been put out of action—the answers to the questions in my mind became clear. In "preparing for the worst" the country was going through another gigantic revolution of a type and scope never attempted by any country in history. I found leaders and people at one in their determination to defend the North and unify the country or die in the attempt. In the pages that follow I have set out how they are going about all this.

WILFRED G. BURCHETT

Phnom Penh, August 1966

Chapter 1

AT GROUND LEVEL

At a Hanoi concert, during the first part of my visit, I met for a moment General Vo Nguyen Giap, North Vietnam's brilliant Defense Minister and Commander in Chief. He knew I had just returned from the coastal areas where the battle for roads and bridges raged daily. "So you've seen what American air power is worth?" he said, adding with a contemptuous laugh: "Nothing!" Later, in a recorded interview he gave his views on this subject in greater detail. From a military viewpoint, his sneer was justified. Otherwise how explain that 18 months after the best American planes and pilots were sent to destroy the few hundred miles of road and railway that lead to the 17th parallel, they were still attacking the same bridges, the same junctions and crossroads, the same radar stations, even the same miniscule targets such as the fishing town of Dong Hoi and the islet of Cong Co, both just north of the 17th parallel?

Traffic rolled down Highway No. 1 almost normally. I found myself moving at almost the same speed as during my last trip toward the 17th parallel, two years previously. I found some of the bridges I had seen in 1964 damaged, others untouched. But I also found more bridges than formerly, including some over rivers where there had never been a bridge before in all of Vietnam's history! American bombing of the traditional ferries made new bridges necessary, and more efficient. They were not the sort of bridges the American pilots were looking for or would find even if they were looking, or could destroy if they did find. The Vietnamese call them floating bridges—a variant of pontoons, except that instead of the roadway being supported by boats, it rested upon huge bundles of unsinkable giant bamboo. Built in easily transportable and joinable sections, they could be assembled quickly at nightfall, towed away at daybreak, and reassembled next evening at any one of a dozen or so crossing points to which branch roads of the main highway now led.

"Our leaders laid down," explained Doan Trong Truyen

from the State Planning Commission, "that transport and communications are the central and most urgent task in wartime. Our slogan must be: 'The enemy destroys, we repair. The enemy destroys again, we repair again and ensure transport and communications.' To achieve this," continued Truyen, "means a bitter fight between us and the enemy. We have a whole army of workers concentrated on this. They not only repair damage; they also build new strategic communications networks, new highways and bridges. We've been able to keep transport moving, both for civilian needs and the war. There was a certain slowing down when the attacks started in February last year until about July when we got organized. From July until now (May 1966) the volume of transport, even from Hanoi to the 17th parallel, is greater than ever before."

For anyone who knows North Vietnam, and I had been visiting the country regularly from the start of the Dien Bien Phu battle in 1954 until my previous visit in 1964, it was evident that what Doan Trong Truyen said was correct. On the major and secondary routes, more traffic was moving than ever before. Not only that, but goods and equipment were arriving on time.

For years past everything connected with the country's economy has been planned, and that includes transport. Today also the transport convoys, from trains and trucks to junks and bicycles, work to a strict timetable. Transport companies enter into pledges to deliver specific volumes of goods at specific places on specific dates. I am assured that the pledges are invariably met even in the most intensively bombed areas. In entering into such pledges, allowance is made for a certain average of time lost due to bomb damage, and this is a fairly precise figure—precise because the road-menders also give pledges and have their plans too. They know how long it will take to repair the maximum damage the bombs can cause on any given sector. With such a system the planners at the center only have to start feeding goods into the transport pipeline in volumes required and on appropriate dates—adding their own margin of error—to have them flowing out in the right quantities, at the right times and places. These were the sort of calculations that General Vo Nguyen Giap had to make for Dien Bien Phu in 1954, under more difficult circumstances when he had to calculate in terms of human backs, ox-carts, bicycles and a single, terrible mountainous road with no organized economy behind him. Nothing that US air power can do, or has been able to do in a very considerable and costly effort so far, can alter this. Washington knows this, despite the optimistic communiques that continue to pour out of Saigon.

"In fact we ought to be 'grateful' to the Americans," continued Doan Trong Truyen of the State Planning Commission. "Their bombs forced us to jump ahead and do things in a few months that would otherwise have taken years. Certainly we did more in 1965 to improve transport and communications than we had done in the previous three or four years. For instance, we had discussed for a long time the question of improving the railroad from Pingshiang on the Chinese frontier. Major improvements were planned for 1965, the last year of the five-year plan. By the end of 1964 we had prepared a plan which provided for these improvements but in the end we shelved it because we felt we had not the manpower available. But when the bombs started to fall, we pulled the plan out of the filing cabinets and the whole job was completed in a little over four months. The improvements are not just a wartime necessity but very important for peacetime developments.

"On one single stretch of railway and highway along the coast, over 2,000 tons of bombs have been dropped and quite small bridges along this stretch have been attacked 20 and more times each. But roads and railways still function normally. Damage is often repaired before the smoke clears away. Our notions of time to repair bridges has changed radically. Normally there would have been lots of paper work. After the expert inspections, estimates of structural damage, various draft projects for the repairs sent to numerous department heads to chew over, reports and recommendations from procurement, financial and other experts would come up to ministerial level. Several ministries would become involved. Paper work alone would take months. Some of our specialists sent to look at a damaged bridge with our old way of looking at things—in the first period of the attacks—said: 'Six months, maybe a year.' But battle-hardened workers on the spot said: 'Nonsense. We'll repair it in a month.' The specialists were scandalized. But, in fact, traffic was moving again within a week. There have been many similar cases. More recently the workers have rationalized, systematized their experiences. With stocks of standardized structural parts which they have designed themselves together with some of our experts, they have repaired or even replaced damaged bridges within one day."

This is very demoralizing for American pilots when reconnaissance photos taken after bridges have been claimed destroyed, show them in place again! A vitally important fact in this is that the repair gangs, often headed by fledgling graduates of the engineering faculty of Hanoi University or Polytechnic Institute, have full authority to go ahead with repairs without any reference to departments or ministries.

In traveling around the country, I noticed many roads that I had never seen before. At times I came across groups of young people, often enough working by the light of blazing bamboo torches or small roadside fires at night, hacking away at rocks and trees, hauling earth in wicker baskets, pushing and pulling at road-rollers, for miles on end. On this, Doan Trong Truyen had the following to say:

"During the past year, new strategic highways have been built between the various zones, and a whole network of new inter-zonal, inter-provincial and inter-district highways and roads have been built, giving us numerous alternate routes in every direction. As with bridge construction and repair, this work has been decentralized. Previously it all came under the Ministry of Communications; now it comes under zonal, provincial and district authorities."

Our road lay through fields of flourishing sweet potatoes, the lush, deep green foliage giving promise of a bumper crop. Water pounded along at a furious rate in a yard-wide irrigation channel, parallel to the road, filtering through at regular intervals to the rows of potatoes. We were approaching the Ban Thach dam.

Suddenly a thought struck me. Shouldn't these be rice fields and not sweet potatoes? There was no lack of water, which sweet potatoes hardly need. And Vietnamese peasants regard the latter as a second-rate crop compared to rice. I asked the district committee chief who was acting as guide.

"Quite correct," he said. "This would normally be rice land. But for months past the Americans have been bombing the Ban Thach dam. It irrigates around 50,000 hectares of rice fields. So far we've been able to save it. They badly damaged the sluice gates once. On another occasion they breached the dike walls, but the peasants rushed out and plugged the breaches. We'll fight to the utmost to save the dam. But if the worst comes to the worst. . . .

"Ever since the first attacks the local co-op members have worked might and main to build subsidiary dams and irrigation systems to trap as much of the water as possible and save it for the rice fields. They have levelled off the fields and raised the terrace banks to trap the water wherever possible. But this bit of land we're passing through now, is too high. If the dam is seriously breached we couldn't get any water here, so we decided to plant it to sweet potatoes—we'll get a food crop off it even if the worst happens."

At the sluice gates and small hydro-electric station, workers were working away at wrecking machines, salvaging undamaged parts, trying to put together one whole machine from two wrecked ones. There were bomb craters all around the sluice gates and the retaining walls, where the water backed up before hurtling down to the turbines. There was nothing remotely resembling a military target within scores of miles. Electricity from the small station powered local irrigation pumps, the dam and power station being exclusively for food production.

At a sister dam at Bai Thuong, two jet fighter-bombers roared over while our little group was actually on the dam embankment. Heavy antiaircraft guns opened up, and little black clouds started immediately scampering after their tails. The roar of the jets and the guns and the crashing explosion of a few bombs they dropped, were merged into almost a single sound. It was all over in a second or two, the planes not diving or circling but hurtling straight ahead in a single, futile bombing run. The bombs crashed into some rice fields and a bamboo thicket, sending up spouts of soil and smoke and carving out huge craters which peasants, who had flattened themselves in the fields as the planes passed, started filling in immediately. A lone sentry on the dam embankment laid aside his rifle as the planes passed, and went back to an enormously long fishing line which stretched down into the seething waters, far below. A hamlet of brick houses, under the trees of which we parked our jeeps, had been bombed to rubble in previous attacks.

On our way back to Thanh Hoa provincial capital, we stopped to examine what was left of the Thanh Hoa tuberculosis hospital No. 71. It had been attacked by 40 jet bombers on July 8, 1965. Forty patients and five doctors were killed and about 50 buildings wiped out. On August 21, 50 more bombers came and completed the work, reducing all remaining buildings to rubble or roofless, windowless ruins. An old man was hurling a fishing net into a water-filled crater in front of what had been a research laboratory; a small boy was herding some ducks into another of the bigger craters. A jagged hole in one of the walls of the X-ray lab marked the passage of a rocket.

The district of Tinh Gia, in Thanh Hoa province, is one of the most heavily bombed regions of North Vietnam as it harbors a crossroads of north-south and east-west communications. At the time of my visit, late in February 1966, it was estimated that one bomb had fallen for every seven inhabitants or one for every 300 square yards approximately. But Tinh Gia had also led the country in food production, the whole district averaging five tons per hectare, individual cooperatives getting up to 7.5 tons. And a Tinh Gia primary school had won national distinction as a "model" school, which means that every pupil in every class had received maximum marks in every subject. In other words, Tinh Gia was the living illustration of the saying, "the more they bomb the more we produce, the better we study."

At the Catholic fishing village of Ba Lan, also part of Tinh Gia district, I found the women very proud of the fact that they had largely replaced the men in the little fleet of fishing sampans; and it was mainly women who were hauling in the fishing nets on the beach, back-breaking work though it is. Despite the occasional attacks and the fact the boats had to fish in the less fertile waters nearer the shore, the 1965 catch was only down by two per cent compared to 1964, while the quantity sold to the state was slightly increased. In the rice fields it was the women who were following on behind the buffalo-drawn ploughs, something without precedent for Vietnam; almost every other one had a rifle or light automatic slung across her back.

In passing, one notes that the young women in the villages have grown more beautiful in recent years. Mainly because they have given up the habit of lacquering their teeth black and their smiles now reveal rows of beautifully white even teeth. But also because even the very slight rise in living standards that 12 years of peace have given them, more plentiful food and better hygiene, have rounded them out slightly and added some color to their cheeks. Full black eyes, pleated black hair often hanging to the waist, delicate skins, symmetrical faces, they manage to remain exquisitely feminine while doing the roughest sort of work—or even when engaged in bayonet drill.

I was taken to the hamlet of Thang Loi, in the Thanh Hoa district of Tho Xuan. Here 360 households, 1,600 inhabitants in all, until recently had farmed 85 hectares, far less land per head than the national average. The previous year 84 families, comprising 420 inhabitants, had moved away to the virgin lands of the northwest. Average crops until 1961 had been around two tons to the hectare for one crop yer year. Then came irrigation from the Ban Thach dam. Immediately there were two crops a year. The co-op management started the intensive use of green fertilizer, mainly provided by a nitrogen-producing sort of green slime now cultivated in many village ponds in North Vietnam. The first five-ton per hectare crop was produced in 1962 and by 1965, the output had been pushed up to 6.9 tons for the whole cooperative. Up till 1961, the hamlet received a yearly subsidy of ten tons of rice from the state. In 1965, Thang Loi sold 39.5 tons of rice to the state instead, after providing a ration of 27 kilograms per head per month for the cooperative members. "Eat our Fill and Beat the US Aggressors," is their slogan, the farm chairman assured me. Thang Loi was the first farm in Thanh Hoa province to attain the goal of five tons per hectare and two pigs per family, and in addition to rice had supplied 22 tons of pigs to the state in 1965.

It is a charming village, streets lined with coconut palms, every house with a garden of fruit trees, oranges, papaya, banana palms, trellises covered with vines of cucumbers and squash, bright splashes of color everywhere from hibiscus, bou-

gainvillea and other tropical flowers. The co-op chairman
started rattling off the changes that had taken place in their
lives. Every house has its own cement-lined well and double
brick-toilet system, every family has two mosquito nets and two
blankets, all adults have pullovers—only landlords and rich
peasants had pullovers before, he reminded me—everyone has
proper spring beds (no longer the old bamboo ones), all the children are in school, and so on. When he mentioned the brick
toilets and the general cleanliness, I was suddenly struck by
something.

Thang Loi and other vanguard hamlets I had visited have
lost their smells. In visiting Vietnamese villages it was often
difficult for westerners to hide their discomfort at the evil, all-
pervading odors that came from open toilets, cesspools and the
rest. The bad smells have gone, or are fast going forever, like
the black lacquered teeth. And this is another of the revolutions
in the Vietnamese countryside. Dr. Pham Ngoc Thach, the ver-
satile and energetic Minister of Public Health, known abroad
for his original work on tuberculosis and at home for the fact
that he is almost always in his laboratories or hospitals or check-
ing up on public health measures in the countryside, drove this
point home when he escorted me to one of his model villages
not far from Hanoi.

At Quang An village Dr. Thach pointed with pride to the fact
that every home had its double-system WC and its cement-lined
wells, and that every inhabitant had complete vaccination or in-
oculation against communicable diseases:

"WC's, wells, vaccination," he said, "these are the three best
means of fighting against chemical and bacteriological warfare."

"Do you think it will come to that?" I asked.

"They are using chemical warfare on a large scale in the
South," replied Dr. Thach, "including the poisoning of water
supplies. We must prepare for the worst." The system of du-
plicate, deep, brick-lined toilets, each with a close-fitting cover,
permitted rotation of use and retaining the excreta in each in
turn for three months before spreading it as the traditional fertilizer in the fields. By this time harmful bacteria are killed, and
smells are abolished from the beginning. As for the individual
wells, Dr. Thach estimated they would make it much more dif-

ficult for the Americans to wreak havoc by air-dropping poison-
ous chemicals into streams and other communal water supplies,
as has happened in South Vietnam. Water reaching into the
wells was sufficiently filtered through the surrounding earth to
eliminate poisons. "We ought to 'thank' the Americans for forcing us to tackle this problem," said Dr. Thach. "They have
stimulated the peasants to complete in a few months what
would have taken us many years of stubborn propaganda campaigns otherwise."

Another source of great pride in the sweet-smelling hamlet of
Thang Loi was the way in which school dispersal had been
handled. This was an obvious necessity. All school buildings in
Thanh Hoa province and the other coastal province I visited,
together with all hospitals and sanatoria, had either been
bombed to smithereens or had been evacuated in expectation
of bombing. Any large building of brick or stone in the countryside was an automatic target for American pilots, doubtless
reported back after the bombings as "barracks, military ware-
houses," and so forth. In Thanh Hoa, provincial authorities had
asked householders to "move closer together" and free some
of their houses as school classrooms, or concentrate the family
in the kitchen for living quarters and leave the rest for classrooms. Especially those families whose homes were best protected from snooping planes by trees were asked to give temporary shelter until new classrooms, which would look as much
as possible like peasant huts, could be built. The population of
Thang Loi had certainly been obliging. And in some cases it
meant walls of homes being cut away to provide more light, not
to mention having the garden dug up to provide communication trenches for the kiddies to rush to the comparative safety of
deep, log-reinforced underground shelters. Communication
trenches started right alongside the desks. In general, classrooms
at Thang Loi were indistinguishable from the peasants' houses
and it was only when one heard the chanting of lessons that one
knew where to look for fragments of an evacuated school.

Apart from the children receiving general education, 60 adult
cooperative members were attending specialized courses in agricultural technique.

Three children of co-op members had graduated from university, one as an electrical engineer, the two others as agronomists, and all three were now back in the village.

The sharp-faced, energetic chairman, rattling off all the blessings of co-operative life, kept the best till the last: "Since October 1965, we have combined with the two other hamlets that make up the village of Xuan Thanh to form a single big co-operative. It combines 812 households, with 3.700 inhabitants and 230 hectares of land. We have 800 draught animals. And we plan to produce the equivalent of 11.5 tons of rice per hectare during 1966, as our contribution to the war against the American aggressors."

"What does equivalent to rice mean?"

"We calculate three tons of sweet potatoes as one ton of rice and we aim to produce 22 tons of potatoes and four tons of rice per hectare. Crop prospects for the fifth month show that it is really possible."

"How are you going to bring about such an increase?"

He ticked off on four fingers: "Water, manure, industriousness, selected seed. Irrigation work has to be carried out according to a very strict agricultural calendar; seedlings have to be planted out precisely on time regardless of enemy air activities. We will spread ten tons of manure per hectare, mainly specially treated human excrement but also green stuff from the ponds. Industriousness means careful work in eliminating every weed, especially in the paddy fields, and great attention to the seedlings before planting them out. As for seed selection, we have an expert selection board in the cooperative itself, supervised by our own specialists who follow courses at a provincial school for seed specialists."

As for labor problems: "Every man between 18 and 40 is enrolled in the 'three-readies' movement (see page 12). Our women are enrolled in the 'three-responsibilities' movement [to replace men at work, encourage husbands and sons to enlist in the armed forces, look after the family]. Ninety per cent of our young men joined in volunteer brigades for work projects or enlisted in the army and it is our women folk who now represent 70 per cent of our labor force. Women do men's jobs and the older men have learned to do what was always a woman's job, planting out the rice seedlings. It is vitally important if you want heavy crops that the seedlings be planted out strictly on time. So everyone lends a hand even if it is dangerous or work must continue day and night."

We tramped over the fields, admiring the sheer beauty of verdant fertility, wherever one looked the endless fields of rice —thick plants in geometric rows between which girls, ankle-deep in mud, were wheeling new mechanical weeders. The rows lead like rays of green light east toward the sea, from which death came so swiftly in the carrier-borne planes of the Seventh Fleet, prowling not so many miles off the coast. On the higher land leading toward the powder-blue mountains of Laos, it was rows of sweet potatoes. Water gurgled away in every direction along the irrigation channels. The special fragrance of growth and fertility, of a soil bursting with vitality, thrusting forth its riches in reward for faithful services rendered. The fields of potatoes stopped a few yards from a railway line. Off to the north, a solitary railway station had been blasted to bits, and two brick houses nearby, probably for the station staff, had also been reduced to rubble. The screaming roar of jets coming from the cloud-tipped Laotian mountains this time brought the self-defense girls running to individual, concrete cylinders embedded in the ground, from where they started aiming at the planes in case they came low. As it happened, they flashed across the sky, a pair of them, well out of range; "reconnaissance," the farm manager said. As we left, our jeep laden down with bananas, papayas, coconuts and lengths of sugarcane, and two enormous carp from the fish-breeding pond, the farm manager said: "You see, there's a real revolution going on in the countryside. If the Americans hadn't started bombing us it would never have gone so fast." One was reminded of the title of an article by the British journalist James Cameron after a visit to North Vietnam: "Every bomb on North Vietnam is a bonus for Ho Chi Minh." Almost every Vietnamese one met testified by living example that this was so.

One of the aspects of the revolution in the countryside that I was to learn of later, was demonstrated in Dr. Pham Ngoc Thach's pilot village of Quang An, near Hanoi. When we arrived at the maternity clinic there, an efficient-looking midwife, with a mouthful of black, lacquered teeth, was giving some very realistic advice to a couple of young women regarding the classic western gadgetry of birth control—family planning is the term used in Vietnam. None of the three seemed embarrassed in the slightest at our arrival during the explanation. The midwife, Dr. Thach explained, was a traditional practitioner, one of hundreds mobilized into the public health service after an eight-months' course in modern hygiene. She was proud to show us her gaily colored chart of vital statistics. In 1962 when family planning was first talked about, she delivered 136 babies to Quang An mothers; 82 the following year, 73 for 1964, 58 for 1965 and she estimated 48 for 1966. Even after a 50-per cent drop in infant mortality, the increase of births over deaths had dropped from 3.46 per cent in 1962 to 1.67 per cent in 1965. This latter figure would be regarded as a satisfactory national level.

The high incidence of births in Vietnam has been a source of official anxiety for years past. In one Catholic hamlet I visited in Hung Yen province in 1963, the average number of children for each of almost 200 families was eleven! But family planning is very much in vogue in the villages today. After the revelation in Quang An, progress in this sphere was added to the list of standard questions I asked in every village and hamlet visited. Later I was to see the results of some very interesting research that the indefatigable Dr. Thach has been pursuing in this field.

One of the most senseless examples of bombing I was to come across in Thanh Hoa province was on the road to Sam Son, a seaside resort where lots of rest homes for workers have been built up in recent years. A few miles before Sam Son itself, there was a fine Old Peoples Home, half a dozen or so red-tiled, brick buildings. It had also been bombed to rubble in a series of raids in July 1965, and doubtless the destruction of another "naval barracks" was registered in the Pentagon records. If it is true, as reported in the American press at the time, that President Johnson personally approved every target to be attacked in North Vietnam to insure that no civilian losses would be incurred, one can only assume that either the President had particularly bloodthirsty moods or American intelligence is pitifully inadequate. Between June 12 and August 22, 1965, eight major hospitals and sanatoria were attacked, many of them repeatedly, until in each case, every building was destroyed.

The attacks on the Quynh Lap leper sanatorium and research center were particularly scandalous. It is difficult to find an excuse for this, even if one accepts that the US is justified in any attacks at all against the DRV with which it is not in a state of war. Dozens of ordinary publicity magazines and scientific journals in the DRV had published photographs of the big leprosorium set out among filao trees on the coast, in Nghe An province. At the time of the first attack on June 12, there were over 2,000 lepers dispersed in some 160 buildings of the sanatorium; 139 of them were killed and 80 seriously wounded. Every day for the following ten days, the attacks were repeated, sometimes several times a day, until virtually nothing was left. Losses were particularly heavy because many of the lepers were cut down by machine-gun bullets as they tried to hobble and crawl to safety on stumps of arms and legs.

As the attack continued day after day, Vietnamese cameramen were able to get to the spot and shoot a horrifying documentary film which shows white-clad attendants with lepers slung across their shoulders, others on stretchers with bombs exploding all around them; bodies blasted off the stretchers, attendants blown off their feet, but recovering their charges and staggering on through the bomb blasts to shelters among the rocks.

If the rubble of the Quynh Lap leper sanatorium and the Thanh Hoa TB hospital are symbols of a ruthless and senseless, to say the least, use of air power, the Ham Rong bridge across the Ma river, at Thanh Hoa, is the symbol of the efficient defiance of the Vietnamese people.

At the time I last crossed it, at the beginning of March 1966, it had withstood many hundreds of attacks; some 3,000-odd bombs had been hurled against it and hundreds of rockets and bull-pup missiles. It is a vital bridge, carrying road and rail traffic on the main north-south communications route. Its defenders claim they had downed 69 planes before the Americans apparently decided to give up. At the time I left North Vietnam, the bridge was still intact, with numerous battle scars on its girders and structural elements, but trains and truck convoys still moved safely across it. I interviewed Commander Denton,

of the US Navy, shot down on his very first mission over North
Vietnam while attacking the Ham Rong bridge. He fell smack
into the Ma river. In the interview (published in a later chapter)
he refused to say what he was attacking or where he fell. But
by chance I had earlier met one of his captors, Nguyen Thi
Hang, the beautiful young woman commander of a local self-
defense unit which had taken part in 30-odd battles defending
the Ham Rong bridge. "He threw away his knife and pistol
while he was still parachuting down," said Nguyen Thi Hang
(Miss Moonlight), "and he went into the river with his hands
up. We fished him out and tied him up."

At first when the word "battle" was employed to describe an
air attack, I objected: "You mean air attack," I said. "No,"
came the reply, "we consider such actions as battles between our
forces and theirs." And when I had the first detailed descrip-
tions of what went on and saw for myself the dispositions taken
and later saw a few actions, then it was clear that "battle" is the
precisely correct term. Every air attack is met with immediate
and fierce resistance: Pilots are correct when they complain they
have to fly down through several levels of fire to get at their
targets. Which explains why they have never smashed the Ham
Rong bridge and dozens of other less important ones against
which they have made scores of attacks.

Any important target is protected by heavy and medium anti-
aircraft guns. But if pilots come down low enough for precision
attacks, they run into a deadly curtain of small-arms fire from
hundreds, sometimes thousands of rifles and light machine guns
in the hands of workers, peasants and students, from the million
or so Vietnamese organized in self-defense units. The dearest
desire of every one of these is to get an American aircraft in
the sights of his weapon. The enemy has been anonymous for
too long. Death has come from afar. There is a feeling of exulta-
tion when the chance comes to fight back. It has become a
nationwide duty to study plane silhouettes, to memorize char-
acteristics of speed and altitude; to recognize planes by their
sounds; to know how many lengths ahead of a certain type one
must aim if it is in level flight and at which point of the nose
to fire if it is dive-bombing.

Can small-arms fire be effective against America's supersonic fighter-bomber? One has only to visit the central plane "ceme-tery" where a certain number of the downed planes have been collected, and examine the wreckage to know that the answer is yes. Many of the wrecks are riddled with holes of various caliber, including ordinary rifle bullets. The curtain of small-arms fire has two major advantages. First, it throws diving planes off their course. At least that seems the only logical explanation for the fact that 70 per cent of the bombs aimed at the Ham Rong bridge fell on the nearby hamlet of Van Phuc, which is now a mass of cratered ruins, while the bridge still stands. The attack-ing pilots, including one of America's greatest aces and bridge destruction experts, downed over the bridge, never held to their dives. They were already pulling out of their dives to avoid the deadly curtain of inter-woven small-arms fire, when they re-leased their bombs. Of those that held to their course, 69 ac-cording to the defenders' figures went on down with their planes or limped out of their dives to fall elsewhere. Only a fraction of the pilots could even use their parachutes. The other ad-vantage of the massed small-arms fire is against planes that skim in from the sea low over the fields for a sneak attack, hoping to avoid radar detection and classic anti-aircraft fire. The fact that tens of thousands of peasants and workers are permanently at defense positions, makes this very difficult. The sheer volume of fire, coming from hands that do not tremble and eyes unafraid to look planes straight in the face, force the sneak-attackers to zoom up to heights where they have to reckon with medium and heavy anti-aircraft guns. The element of surprise is lost.

In their attacks, the Americans are caught between various contradictions. To bomb with precision requires slow, propeller-driven planes, which can turn in relatively tight circles and go on down to place their bombs—if not with the same precision as the guerrillas can plant their plastics, at least fairly precisely on their targets. But such planes are dream targets for the anti-aircraft gunners and even North Vietnam's embryo air force. To avoid the heavy losses they took in the first months of the air-ground battles, and even to avoid the handful of MIG-17's which the North Vietnamese send up from time to time, the Americans are forced to send their fastest fighter-bombers. Flying high and fast over their targets, usually in a single run, these are incapable of precision bombing. They try and compensate for this by dropping huge quantities of bombs indiscriminately with the hope that the law of averages will come to their aid and some will hit the target. The same is true of the B-52 bombers so far used against North Vietnam.

The first much publicized raid, "the biggest of the war," was against the Mu Gia pass where Route No. 12 leads into Laos. The pass and road were said to have been smothered with bombs, artificial landslides provoked, the road put out of action. Vietnamese on the spot told me that in fact 109 bombs were dropped of which four fell on the road, the rest exploding in the jungle. The road was cleared within a few hours, a fact the Americans seem to have recognized only two weeks later when they discovered the road was still functioning and bombed it again, with the same negligible results.

But what the pilots miss with their bombs is certainly made up for by the paper work of those who draft communiques. I was astonished to read an item in *The New York Times* of May 9, 1966, quoting the American military spokesman in Saigon as saying that all railroads and highways leading into Hanoi had been cut and the capital was isolated: "Most of the arteries were sliced in a series of air raids in mid-April, the spokesman said, but what the military considered the final import link, the highway and railroads running northeast to Nanning, China was blocked yesterday (Sunday, May 8)."

May 7 was, in fact, the day I left Hanoi, and I have no way of knowing whether a "highway and railroad" running northeast to China was "blocked." I have good reason to believe that if it were "blocked" on Sunday it would have been "deblocked" by Monday. But as for the rest, between mid-April and the early days of May, I was traveling almost daily in all directions from Hanoi and all roads and railroads were functioning normally. There were a dozen or so other correspondents also traveling around and I never heard of a single case of any "arteries" being "sliced."

If American taxpayers could see the military results of the fabulous expenditure of their money by American air power in North Vietnam they would be shocked to the core, at least to their pocketbooks, even if they were not affected by the moral aspects of it all. For expert American justification of General Giap's contemptuous "Nothing!" there was an article in the April 5, 1966, number of *Look* magazine by General Matthew B. Ridgeway who commanded the United Nations forces in Korea and presumably knows his subject.

"Korea," he writes, "also taught that it is impossible to interdict the supply routes of an Asian army by air power alone. We had complete air mastery over North Korea, and we clobbered Chinese supply columns unmercifully. Unquestionably, we inflicted serious damage upon the Chinese and greatly complicated their problems of reinforcement and supply. But we did not halt their offensive nor materially diminish its strength. The Chinese, like the Vietnamese, traveled light, with each man carrying his ammunition, his food and his weapon on his back. . . . In Korea, I saw whole sections of railroad bombed into scrap iron by aircraft and yet the enemy rebuilt the tracks in a single night and the trains ran the next day. . . . It is easy for the civilian mind to be seduced with talk of 'easy' conquest through air power. But the crucial battles are still won by foot soldiers. . . ."

As I was on the receiving end of US air power in Korea for two years, traveling up and down the main supply route which led from Sinanju, on Korea's Yalu river frontier with China, down towards Kaesong-Parmunjom, at least 20 times while covering the Parmunjom cease-fire talks, I know that what General Ridgway now discloses is correct. Moreover, the daily Air Force communiques on destruction of truck convoys were a source of hilarious amusement to the Koreans and Chinese. Time and again when the Air Force claimed to have destroyed 300 or 400 trucks, not a single vehicle was hit. During my 20-odd night rides over that route, I saw only a single truck hit and that was on my first trip. Traffic moved at night and although the night bombers were always around, bombing and strafing at something or other, they were useless. And having been on the receiving end of American air power in both South and North Vietnam, I can add my snort of "Nothing," as far as military results are concerned in Vietnam, to that of General Giap and it seems of General Ridgway also.

Implicit admission of the failure of American air power to disrupt communications was made by Defense Secretary McNamara in giving the reasons for the strikes against the fuel depots in the Hanoi-Haiphong areas at the end of June 1966. "Enemy truck movements to South Vietnam doubled during the first five months of 1966 compared with the same period in 1965," he said. "Further, the daily tonnage of supplies moved overland has increased 150 per cent, and personnel infiltration 120 per cent during 1966, compared with 1965 averages. This has led to a greater reliance on petroleum." This greatly increased north-south movement of supplies took place despite the 15 months of day and night bombing of bridges and communications routes. It seems predictable that the bombing of fuel depots will take its routine place in the daily communiques, along with the bridges destroyed, the roads and railway lines cut. It may well be that within a year of the strikes against the Hanoi-Haiphong fuel depots, there will be an attempt to justify another mad escalation effort by claiming that the movement of supplies has doubled again as compared to 1966.

The absurdity of American claims was perhaps never better illustrated than by President Johnson's solemn announcement that in that single, first raid on June 29, 1966, 57 per cent of North Vietnam's fuel reserves had been destroyed. By what fantasies of American intelligence such a precise figure was arrived at—when the pilots themselves stated that smoke prevented assessment of results—only President Johnson could know. In fact, the major part of North Vietnam's fuel reserves, for many months previous to the strikes, had been distributed throughout the country, deep underground and well out of reach of American bombs or rockets. Attacks against the Hanoi-Haiphong depots had been anticipated ever since the first bombings of the North took place in February 1965.

If President Johnson and his Pentagon experts believe that leaders as experienced as the North Vietnamese would leave 57 per cent of their fuel supplies in the exposed Hanoi-Haiphong depots, they are making the same woeful miscalculations that have marked every stage of their escalation policy.

Only seven weeks earlier, Pentagon and Saigon spokesmen were claiming that all road and rail links with Hanoi had been severed. But in his press conference to justify the raids against Hanoi-Haiphong, McNamara had discovered that "the enemy's military effort is further attested to by his action to improve infiltration-network routes. Some of these routes are new, some have been up-graded for all-weather truck use. By-passes have been built and bamboo-trellised canopies have been rigged over some jungle roads to inhibit aerial observation." And as for previous predictions that the air strikes in the North would force the "Vietcong" in the South to break up into smaller units and go back to guerrilla warfare, McNamara said that "as a result of the greatly increased movement of men and supplies by trucks and powered junks [the latter despite the presence of the mighty Seventh Fleet in Vietnamese waters] there has been a shift from a small-arms guerrilla action to a quasi-conventional military operation involving major supplies, weapons and heavier equipment."

It was not only on the military front that the American bombings proved ineffective. On the civilian front life and work continued normal. Despite the greatly stepped-up raids during May 1966, the spring harvest was reaped, transported and stored, deliveries to the state completed strictly according to the planned timetable.

General Ridgway, incidentally, in the article previously cited also touched on the moral problem, questioning "The increasingly significant ignoring by our planners of the consequences of omitting the moral factor in considering the use of the immense destructive capability which now exists in the world. . . ." And, he adds, "It is my firm belief that there is nothing in the present situation or in our code that requires us to bomb a small Asian nation 'back into the Stone Age'. . . . There must be some moral limit to the means we use to achieve victory."

The Vietnamese would certainly question that American air power could ever "achieve victory," but General Ridgway deserves credit for having touched on the moral aspects of a situation in which the mightiest industrial and military power in the world uses its destructive power against a small, poor and technically backward country like Vietnam.

Chapter 2

AT AIR LEVEL

What do the American pilots think about this? I had fairly long talks with some of them, after they were shot down, and in three cases I recorded verbatim the text of our conversations. Shorn of their wings, down on the ground and prisoners with a very uncertain future, they are obviously not in a very happy frame of mind. But neither are they, it seems, very happy at their bases or aircraft carriers. François Sully, for instance, writing from the aircraft carrier *Kitty Hawk* in *Newsweek*, February 14, 1966, relates that:

"Despite this justifiable pride in a dangerous assignment, many of the Navy pilots were visibly reluctant to be interviewed by visiting newsmen. When pressed for an explanation, they confided that they feared such publicity might lead to harassment against their families by anti-war organizations in the U.S. Admitted one press-shy Navy commander: 'Our biggest morale problem aboard this ship is crank mail, mud letters and threatening phone calls to fliers' wives, parents or relatives at home.'

"And significantly, every time a correspondent tried to approach a pilot, the chief information officer of the *Kitty Hawk* quickly interjected: 'Wouldn't you rather not have your name published or picture taken?' As a result a visitor was left with the odd impression that these tough, professional Navy men were more terrified by the thought of retribution from Stateside Vietniks than from the guns of the Communist enemy."

As a war correspondent covering the Pacific in World War II, I spent a lot of time aboard American aircraft carriers and, as a non-combatant observer, I flew on several combat missions. There were no problems of morale those days. On the contrary. I saw pilots take off in the Battle of the Philippine Sea on missions against the Japanese fleet, at extreme range, knowing there was at least an even chance that they would not make it back to the carriers. And on one occasion I saw them come back, at dusk, fuel tanks exhausted, in such a heavy fog that turning the carriers into the wind to receive the planes was a cumbersome, hazardous business and the landing of the planes even more so. We watched the red and green wing-tip lights of a dozen or more planes circle and circle around the mother ships as the latter fought to get into the wind, saw them come lower and lower until they disappeared into the sea. From the pilots who were picked up, never a complaint; nor from those who took off next morning on similar missions. Their reward was the destruction of the major part of the Japanese Navy.

Pilots those days were only too happy to talk to journalists; only too happy to have their names and photos and exploits published, especially in the home-town press. Why the difference today? It is obvious that those who think at all are ashamed of the role they and their country are playing.

Fernand Gigon, the Swiss journalist, in his book *Les Américains Face Au Vietcong* (Flammarion, Paris, 1965; pages 151–52) relates one hushed-up aspect of the rebellious frame of mind of at least some of the pilots and the fears of their superiors that this might become contagious. He speaks of the scruples of some of the officers at the destruction of villages, rice crops, and human beings burned to cinders: " 'This is no longer war,' say those officers with scruples, 'it's genocide.' Extreme moral confusion and religious convictions lead them to the verge of revolt. They demand that their superior officers release them from their engagement. Headquarters, taken by surprise by these objectors, reminds them of their contracts and their duties as volunteers. It acknowledges, however, not the moral reasons that prompt them (the pilots) to renounce their pledges, but the technical factors that could turn them into poor marksmen, inefficient pilots and, finally, bad Americans. From the strictly military viewpoint these cases border on treason.

"Headquarters makes these conscientious objectors sign a new declaration, according to the terms of which the pilots pledge that on their return to the USA they will neither divulge the reasons for their quitting, nor any scenes of which they have been witness, nor any information that even remotely concerns the war. Then without any fuss the officer is immediately stripped of his rank and his military privileges are taken

away. He returns to his country more alone than if he were in
the middle of the desert. Some turn up in psychiatric clinics.

"Many others, who do not have the courage to break their
contracts, count the days to their release. For them D-Day is
the day of their liberation, that is to say 365 days after they
signed up. Unless, of course, the Senate decides otherwise."

The first of the pilots with whom I had a formal interview was
Lt.-Commander Arthur Vohden, of the US Navy, an operations
officer from the aircraft carrier *Hancock* who was flying an
A4D-1 bomber when he was shot down. Thirty-six years of age,
tall, slim and blond, his leg was in a plaster cast from a serious
injury, requiring bone grafts, when he crashed down on a pile
of rocks. He was dressed in khaki trousers and a blue pullover,
escorted by an armed Vietnamese NCO to the room where the
interview was to take place. After introductions and my asking
him if he had any objections to being interviewed, he told me
he was shot down on April 3, 1965, while on a bombing mission, probably by small-arms fire. His target was the Do Len
bridge in Thanh Hoa province (a bridge that was still intact
in May 1966, more than a year later). This was his fourth
bombing mission. He was captured within five minutes after
landing on a pile of rocks.

"I noticed my leg hanging down," he said. "It was on a hill,
a hill probably 200 feet high. Two Vietnamese men came at
me. They had large knives. They pointed them at my neck.
Of course, they immediately saw my foot. They realized there
was nothing I could do."

"Why do you think they pointed at your neck?" I asked.

"I think it was to indicate that I was their captive."

"Many more Vietnamese people came," Vohden continued.
"They carried me down to the bottom of the hill. They used
sticks. They put sticks under my back and under my legs and
under here (indicating his buttocks). There must have been
about ten of them. They carried me down to the bottom of
the hill.

"After that I lay at the bottom of the hill, I guess for about
an hour. Then more people gathered around. They looked at
me. Some of them appeared to be very angry. Several spat at
me. An elderly man appeared. I thought he had a gun, he

pointed it at me. I could see how the crowd was excited. Then a younger man came up. I could hear them talking, arguing. Apparently he stopped whatever might have happened.

"After that I was carried about 300 yards to a small hut. There some Vietnamese put a splint on my leg. I was there for about one and a half hours. Then I was taken on a stretcher, I guess about 200 to 300 yards. People were lined up alongside the road. I was put in a truck, then taken I don't know where. It was getting dark. I was tied down to the stretcher and the stretcher was wired to the truck. We drove I guess another 15 or 20 minutes. I was taken out of the truck and carried on the stretcher with torches on either side. I was carried up a hill again, lined with what appeared to be hundreds of people. They appeared to be quite angry again. Then I was put on a truck again and taken to what looked like a barracks. After I was there for a short time, a Vietnamese man came in. He told me he was a medical doctor. I could understand that and the word 'Operation'. Shortly after that he put me on a table. Then they gave me ether. . . ."

"Have you had medical treatment since?"

"Yes, sir. I had another operation on May 11 and that's when they cut a piece of bone out."

"What about food?"

"The food is adequate to sustain life. We have a small portion of meat and spinach and cabbage, small portions of this. A small loaf of bread with every meal and water."

"Have you been able to communicate with your family at all?"

"Yes, sir. I have written to my wife once."

"Have you had a reply?"

"Yes, sir. I received two letters from my wife."

"Well, what do you feel now about the war in general? There is, of course, something that troubles most correspondents who come to visit this place. There is an enormous amount of destruction of hospitals, schools, sanatoria and so forth. I served on several US aircraft carriers as a war correspondent in the war against Japan. I remember the targets were very specific. Here, to say the very least, you have been very careless about targets?"

"This, I don't know sir. I was shot down on April 3, and there had been very few bombing missions at that time. Since that time, I can't say. I've only heard what the radio says. I would say that I don't think any of this is planned. In fact I'm sure it's not. I don't know whether it is happening."

"Of course, it is happening. Some of the worst of it, it's true, did happen after you were shot down. But there has been tremendous destruction. It is difficult for us journalists to understand, because you fly reconnaissance missions and there's no excuse for 'mistaken' targets. What is your status here, your legal status?"

"I don't know. We are told that we are war criminals. That's what we are told."

On that note our conversation ended.

Very different to the rather woe-begone, taciturn Lt.-Commander Vohden was 44-year-old Major Lawrence Guarino of the 44th Squadron, 18th Wing of the US Air Force. Although Guarino did not admit it, his captors knew from his documents and flight maps that he was stationed at Korat in Thailand and it was from the US air base there that he had taken off for his bombing missions. Major Guarino, a short, smiling man, was very much at his ease and had no objection to taking part in a filmed, recorded TV interview. He was dressed like Vohden in khaki trousers and blue pullover. He was shot down on June 14, 1965, while on a bombing mission in Son La province. This was his seventh mission.

"How were you shot down?" I asked.

"Well, it was a very bad day. The weather was very low. The target was very heavily defended. As I rolled in to dive, many guns fired at me. I knew I was going to be hit and I was. I was hit very badly, quite a number of times."

"Have you had World War II experience? Or Korea?"

"Yes, World War II. In Southern Europe, Italy. Then China."

"How did the anti-aircraft fire here compare with that in World War II?"

"I think this fire is about as rough as you could find anywhere."

"How long after you were shot down were you captured?"

"Oh, just a matter of minutes. Perhaps 15 or 20."

"Your plane was hit while you were still in your dive?"

"Yes, sir. All the way in the dive. And again as I pulled away from the target I received a very bad hit from an explosive shell and the aircraft went out of control. At that air speed I was able to fly away from the immediate target. Perhaps 10 or 20 miles before I had to leave the aircraft."

"Were you captured by militia or the local population?"

"Both militia and local people."

"How has the treatment been since capture?"

"Alright, very decent. The food has been adequate."

"One of the big questions for us all in the West is what do you think of this war?"

"Of course you get another view when you're inside, looking at it from there. I've prayed many times that both sides, or as many sides as are interested in it, will come to some reasonable solution in the very near future."

"As journalists, we've been given facilities by the authorities to travel around—the destruction of non-military targets is very impressive. Hospitals, schools, sanatoria. I served with some of your people, Air Force and carrier-borne planes, in World War II. The bombing was strictly military. But this time, a great deal of it is non-military. How do you feel about this? How does one explain it?"

"Well, if this is true—and you say you've seen it—then I'm sure that the pilots certainly believe that the targets are military. Any military information that is given, photos if any, certainly show that the targets are military. From what I've read, declarations by our President, the targets are certainly not people. If what you say is true, then it is really by accident. I can't imagine an American pilot attacking a village or a hospital."

"There's no state of war between the USA and North Vietnam. There's been no declaration of war. There's the question of how you feel about taking part in this sort of action?"

"Of course I'm not taking much of a part any more. But you've heard the old saying: 'Ours is not to reason why. Ours is but to do and die.' And we hope and pray that our military and our leaders are doing the right thing, that the President and the people backing him are on the right road. We are directed and ordered to fly missions and don't question this.

We do our duty. That's the position of any Air Force pilot."

"How were you treated from the moment of capture?"

"The people were very decent. Much like people in any country, in fact. It certainly struck me that they were well briefed and knew exactly what to do when they encountered an enemy pilot. I was tied up very securely. I was given water and rice and given very decent treatment."

"What is your status? I mean in view of the fact that there is no state of war, no declaration of war? How do you consider your status here? And how do the authorities consider your status?"

"Well, sir, people here feel that inasmuch as we have attacked targets within this country and as there is no state of war, they feel our acts against them are criminal and we are considered as war criminals. However, we don't consider ourselves to be criminals. Obviously, we consider ourselves to be prisoners of war. However, I'm afraid we are not in much of a position to make a decision on this."

"Have you been able to have any news of your family?"

"Yes, sir. As a matter of fact I received two letters. One written November 1, the other on March 2. I've been able to answer both."

"March 2 of this year?"

"Yes, I've been a prisoner over 11 months."

"How do you feel about the fact that you are taking part in attacking the territory of a country with which your country is not really at war?"

"I don't know why they don't consider themselves as being at war because they certainly are. This seems to me to be only a technicality. I certainly consider that I was at war. I certainly felt that as part of the US Air Force, I was attacking enemy territory. The thought never entered my mind that I was a criminal. I thought I was just carrying out the orders of my superiors and I still feel that way. I believe that. I don't think any of us or our people back home will understand why we should be considered as criminals regardless of whether there is a formal declaration of war, which as I see it, seems to be just a technicality."

At this point I mentioned the Nuremberg verdicts, the fact

that aggression was listed as a crime and that the plea "I only carried out the orders of my superiors" was rejected as a valid argument for the defense. And with Gigon's interesting revelations in mind, I asked: "I wonder what your fellow-pilots, your colleagues felt about this? Didn't they ever query as to whether there was something wrong about these missions?"

"Well, sir, I wouldn't say so. I'm sure they felt they were attacking only military targets."

"There have been several western correspondents here," I pointed out. "Everyone is appalled at the destruction of non-military targets. Quite big hospitals and sanatoria have been bombed time and again, until there is just nothing left. The big leper hospital for instance was bombed 11 or 12 times within as many days."

"Isn't it obvious," Guarino replied, "that no American pilot would attack a hospital if he had the slightest idea that that is what it was? I would say that if so that must be a very grave error in the intelligence service. I'm convinced that they couldn't repeatedly attack areas like that unless they were sure it was a military target. What's to be gained by bombing a hospital?"

"But isn't there this question?" I interposed. "Do pilots have the right to question the target at all? You are given a target, you are given a photo. Suppose you say: 'Well it seems to me that's not an anti-aircraft position, not a bridge, not a barracks. That looks to me like a civilian target.' Do you have the right to question the mission?"

"You certainly have the right to inquire what a target is," he replied. "If you have a photo you can certainly spot anti-aircraft positions. But I say a pilot would not attack a hospital. There must be a gross error if this is so."

I told him again of the destruction of hospitals and schools, the ruins of which I had seen. "I'd say that on the coastal areas, everything that was built in brick or stone, built up by the people here since the war against the French—of all this, nothing is left. This is the inescapable opinion of all who have visited these areas. This is what bothers us. But you think all this must be by mistake?"

"Oh, certainly, sir. The pilots just would not do it if they had the slightest idea that anything like that was happening.

As I said, on our side of it, we like to think that our people are very competent also and no senior officer or commander thinks of anything else than hitting military targets. There's no reason for it."

"Suppose a 'mistake' is made, does someone get punished for it? I mean 'mistake' in inverted commas. A hospital has been bombed. Does the pilot get blamed? Or the operations' officer? The intelligence officer or the commanding officer?"

"No, sir. It has nothing to do with what they call the delivery weapons agency. The lower unit has nothing to do with it because they didn't select the target anyway. These things are hashed out at a higher level. It certainly has nothing to do with us."

"How do you see your future here?"

"I certainly hope that in the future, the people involved will work out a peaceful and reasonable solution. Of course, I as a prisoner am not in a position to do anything but pray for a quick solution."

"What sort of food do you get?"

"We get bread with every meal; soup with greens and vegetables, potatoes and a small meat dish—that's the standard type meal."

"Anything special for Christmas?"

"At Christmas I was able to see a Vietnamese Catholic priest. He spoke French and Latin, but I was able to speak to him through an English-language interpreter, and have a long chat. I'm a Catholic. Christmas dinner was excellent. We had some turkey. For the Vietnamese New Year they also laid on a special meal."

And Major Guarino, still smiling, was escorted away by his armed guard.

TV viewers all over the world, including the United States, saw and heard the interviews with Vohden and Guarino. For prisoners of 13 and 11 months respectively, there is no question but that they were in good physical and mental condition. By their frank defense of their own country's position, their denial of the bombing of hospitals and schools, it was clear that they were not under the influence of any "brain-washing." The TV viewers could themselves compare the appearance of these two officers, and its implications, with what they saw on their TV screens of the barbarous treatment of "Vietcong" prisoners in the South at the hands of American and South Vietnamese troops.

Mention by crack pilots Vohden and Guarino of captors with knives and swords reminded me of one of the most bizarre, but deeply symbolic, scenes I witnessed during my visits to the North. A procession of rubber-tired ox-carts winded its way along a road. Underneath the leafy camouflage, were the remnants of a supersonic F-105 fighter-bomber. Robust peasant girls escorted the little convoy, rifles slung behind them. Following the last cart, a tall, white-bearded old peasant carried the type of spear his ancestors used to repel the Mongols. The convoy was on its way to deposit one more exhibit at the central plane cemetery.

The scene symbolized for me not only the terribly unequal combat but also the confrontation between technique and morale, between men and machines. How many of America's highly trained, top-flight pilots have ended their careers, after a few missions over North Vietnam, with knives or spears at their throats! Their's is as ignominious an end to a career as that of the Phantoms and Thunderchiefs, and other fine creations of the US aircraft industry, tossed aside on village scrapheaps for peasants to come and spit at.

Commander Jeremiah Denton of the US Navy, mentioned earlier as having been downed over the Ham Rong bridge, was a different type than the previous two pilots questioned. Big, tough and somber, he seemed very sure of the righteousness of the course he and his country were pursuing, the "cause" they were defending. As a senior officer, it was clear that he identified himself completely with Pentagon policies. His only regret seemed to be that US air power was not being used to its full capacity, or at least not up to the time he was shot down.

He was shot down on July 18, 1965, by ground fire, on his first bombing mission. His parachute pack was hit and he came down hard, in a river. Immediately, people came in boats, hooked on to his raft and towed him to the shore, where there were others with rifles.

"What is your actual status now?" I asked.

"I'm a captive of the Democratic Republic of Vietnam."

"How is the treatment?"

"The food is adequate. Clothing is provided. (He wore a light, khaki uniform, close buttoned at the neck, with a number printed in black on the tunic.) They take care of any serious problems."

"What do you mean by serious problems?"

"If you get sick, you get medicine."

"What do you think of the situation, now you've been captured for around 10 months?"

"I hope God's will will be done and I fully support my Government in whatever they do."

"About your legal status: In view of the fact that there is no state of war, has this question been raised?"

"They have raised many, many times the question of legal status. I am not considered a prisoner of war."

"What do you think yourself, in view of the fact that there is no state of war, that there has been no declaration of war?"

"I'm in their hands. According to my knowledge there has been no declaration of war during the past 20 years. In other cases prisoners have received POW treatment. I'm not receiving that kind of treatment."

"What do you yourself feel about this?"

"I don't see anything wrong from the US point of view. If there had been a declaration of war, the US would have handled this situation much more severely than what we have tried to carry out."

"As a correspondent, I have seen that many hospitals, sanatoria, schools, etc. have been destroyed. How do you feel about that?"

"I know nothing of that type of destruction. At the time I was free, bombing was restricted to military targets. That's all I can say."

"All those of us who have visited the North have seen many non-military targets destroyed. There's no question about this."

"Certainly not to my knowledge."

"Attacking a country without a declaration of war seems a

very serious business. Did you and your colleagues not raise this point?"

"As I said, during the past 20 years there have been no declarations of war. In Korea there was not. At Suez there was not. In this case there were plenty of warnings. No underhand methods. No sneak attack."

"Apart from the question of the legality or otherwise of attacking an independent country—and a number of your Senators are worried about this—there is this question of attacking non-military targets."

"To my knowledge targets were very strictly limited, to bridges and roads, others like that. President Johnson said that we're not there to try and kill Vietnamese people, only to attack steel and concrete."

"There's too much evidence to the contrary. Gigon, the Swiss journalist, has written a book in which he says that some flyers refused missions because of this. They were eventually discharged on condition—they had to sign a document—that they did not reveal the reason for their discharge or the atmosphere aboard their carriers. Did you hear anything of this?"

"I never heard of anything like this. I can't believe it happened in my unit. I consider we are engaged in a restrained action so far. Under present conditions I must continue to support our action."

"Have you a family? And if so have you had any contact?"

"Yes, I have a wife and seven children. I have written one letter and I have received two replies."

"How has treatment been in relation to what you expected? I assume you all have briefings as to approximately how you will be treated. How does reality compare with the briefings?"

"Until recently, about what I expected. I am not accorded the status of POW. They had been saying that we would not be accorded status of POW."

"I do not think they were saying that at the time you were shot down. This policy was announced much later."

"Yes, they had been saying we would get 'good treatment as they were humanitarians,' but that we would not be considered as POW's."

"How is the food?"

"We get a soup which is quite nourishing. We have side dishes, usually vegetables with some meat. We get bread, French-type bread, good bread. For that '*Vive la France.*'"

And the nearest approach to a smile spread over Commander Denton's face at the thought of the good French bread. Our conversation ended at that. The Commander was so sure his country was right and he was right and God was right and on his side. And that the US Air Force, in fact, should be punishing North Vietnam more severely. With all three pilots there was the "Quiet American" sort of moral conviction that anything their country was doing, including bloody murder, was right and proper and theirs "not to question why," as Major Guarino had put it.

It will be recalled that Major Guarino's documents showed that his bombing mission originated at the US air base at Korat in Thailand. Another captured pilot, Lt.-Colonel Robinson Risner, a veteran of the Korean war and an experienced American ace, was shot down on the morning of September 16, 1965, while attacking the Thanh Rong bridge. Commander of Tactical Squadron 67 of the 18th Tactical Wing, he himself admitted that he had also taken off from Korat in Thailand. The same admission was made by Captain Charles Boyd, who was captured when his F-105 was shot down while in North Vietnam on April 23, 1966. Here is concrete evidence, if more is needed, that Thailand is engaged in acts of war against the Democratic Republic of Vietnam. Under international law, lending one's bases to a third country for aggression against a neighbor is a clear "act of war." If it chooses, North Vietnam has every legal right to invade Thailand and occupy or destroy the bases from which "acts of war" are launched against it, or call upon an ally to do so. Evidence is also on hand that air bases in Laos are being used for a similar purpose, and it is no secret that US planes based in Thailand attack daily that portion of Laos which is controlled by the Pathet Lao. The government of North Vietnam has given a number of warnings to Thailand as to the eventual consequences.

Toward the end of April 1966, there was considerable excitement all over North Vietnam as the scoreboards for planes shot down, set up in public places in every town and village, crept up toward the 1,000-mark. There was intense competition between provinces and batteries, even between the anti-aircraft gunners and MIG fighters, for the glory of bringing down the 1,000th plane. If the Americans noted unusual activity by the handful of MIG's of North Vietnam's infant air force around that time, the competition for the 1,000th plane was at least one of the reasons. Mock targets were built, decoys were set all over the place to attract planes toward this or that battery, district or province. Isolated MIG-17's tried to lure Phantoms in pursuit to give the few MIG-21's the chance of a "kill." As it happened, the 1,000th plane was knocked down by ground fire in Tay Nguyen province, the veteran revolutionary base of the first resistance war against the French.

On the question of the numbers of planes shot down, I found that among the foreign community in Hanoi, mainly diplomats and journalists, while not all conceded that Hanoi's claims were completely correct, they were unanimous that the Hanoi figures were much closer to the truth than those put out by the Americans. Authorities with whom I discussed the matter insisted that their figures were minimal and actual losses are higher than the 1,020-odd claimed by the time I was leaving Hanoi. A personal directive from President Ho Chi Minh laid it down that in order to maintain the confidence that the public has in its government, figures of planes shot down must be strictly accurate. No plane could be considered downed, or included in the day's total, unless the wreckage had been located and "hands laid on it."

I was told that in the early days of the fierce assaults against bridges, reports from the various provinces one day showed 14 planes downed. The High Command was claiming 11, but by the time the communique was to be prepared for the morning press, "hands had not been laid" on a single wreckage. According to the very strict regulations none could be claimed. The responsible officer telephoned President Ho, explaining that to say no planes were downed when various batteries knew they had shot down a plane would also be a blow to confidence in the government. President Ho replied: "You can publish one plane downed." While the communique was being prepared, a UPI despatch from Saigon admitted that four had been downed. Another telephone call to President Ho; he agreed that four could be claimed. As the communique was being adjusted, a Washington announcement came in admitting that eight had been lost. President Ho said: "In that case I'll give you six." This was the figure published and next day Washington scaled its figure down to six.

If the wreckage is not found within two days, the plane is not claimed and claims are only allowed for planes that crash on the territory of the DRV or within territorial waters so that the fishermen can bring in some remnants. "We know there are 88 wrecks around the base at Danang in the South," an officer who prepares the communiques told me. "These are planes that were hit and did not make it back to their carriers."

I asked whether any system had been detected by which the Americans announced or did not announce their losses and I was told that it had been noted that if a plane was downed and the pilot parachuted out, the loss would not be announced if the Americans thought there was any chance of rescuing the pilot. Later they would announce the loss if it were an important pilot, a major or above, but if he were "small fry" the loss would not be announced. Also they usually announced losses of planes that crashed into the sea if they succeeded in picking up the pilot. It is significant that the Americans report almost as many pilots "believed captured" as they admit planes downed, whereas in fact the vast majority of planes were shot down in dive-bombing raids in which the pilots crashed with their planes.

As we were about to set out and film scenes of a "quiet Sunday afternoon in Hanoi"—it was April 17—there were violent explosions that made the hotel windows shudder, and then the incredible roar of jets, such as one was used to in the provinces but not in Hanoi. Within split seconds, girls with red arm bands had rushed into the room to close windows and try and persuade us to go down into the shelters. It was the first raid on the capital's outskirts. No alert had been sounded, but the explosion of bombs and heavy anti-aircraft guns continued.

I watched the people in the streets. They hurried, ran in fact, mothers with babes in their arms, but there was no panic, no confusion. I never heard a single shout or wail. Within a flash everyone was out of sight, except a few laggards in the self-defense units, belatedly rushing to their gun positions. The red flag of danger had been hoisted on an adjacent bank building. On many roofs surrounding the hotel, I noticed barrels of anti-aircraft batteries pointed skyward, the binoculars of the lookouts pointed in the same direction as the guns. As usual it was over within seconds. The bombs fell near an agricultural institute in the outskirts, two little girls playing on a sandheap were killed by a rocket. Because of the dense anti-aircraft fire the pilots had not pressed their attacks at whatever were their real targets. But is was a warning.

Much of Hanoi had been evacuated at the end of 1965, but as no raids took place, people started filtering back in the first months of 1966. After the Sunday raid, evacuation started in earnest again, especially as three days earlier jet bombers had taken a run down the main street of the textile town of Nam Dinh, killing over 100 people and wounding hundreds more. After the first heavy attacks against the big textile plant, the main industry in Nam Dinh, the population of 95,000 had been cut back to 35,000. But as always happens, people tend to drift back and casualties in the April 14 raid were needlessly high. At the same time as Hanoi's outskirts were bombed for the first time, the town of Phu Ly, 50 miles southwest of Hanoi, was also bombed. A few days later, it was the outskirts of Haiphong.

A new stage of "escalation" had been reached. The following Sunday, April 24, at 6 P.M., just as people were coming out of church at Phat Diem, the main Catholic center in North Vietnam, the bombers skimmed in low over the sea and made a devastating sneak attack. One church was completely destroyed. Many of those hastening out of it, especially women and children, were killed. Phat Diem is known for three things: It is an important fishing center; it has the largest Catholic Cathedral in North Vietnam, and it is a famous center for rush mats, baskets and all sorts of woven handicrafts. I had visited it several times in 1955–57 and again in late February 1966. It was one of those towns where changes had been most marked, rows of new brick houses, many new bridges over the river that ran parallel with the main street. Old acquaintances pressed forward to tell me how life had prospered in recent years, with the fish catch much heavier and better marketing for their handicraft articles, and with all the children at school. I was taken to see the improved fishing boats. Now Phat Diem lies pretty much in ruins. It was mainly a one-street town and the bombers had made their bombing and strafing run along the entire length of that one main street—scrupulously clean and gay with colored mats and baskets when I last drove along it.

For the next few days after the first attack on Phat Diem, the planes concentrated on the fishing fleet, day after day reporting hundreds of junks and sampans of a "supply convoy" sunk. Phat Diem seems to have been given its *coup de grace* on Saturday, May 7, when the American communique on air activities reported that "three waves of aircraft had attacked the naval base of Phat Diem." Naval base! The term must have been a great surprise to those inhabitants of Phat Diem still alive to hear it. A pretentious name for a small fishing town, whose beaches could not handle any vessel bigger than a small fishing smack. "Seventeen buildings were destroyed and eight burned," the communique continued, "two explosions were observed."

Chapter 3

CRIME AND PUNISHMENT

The North Vienamese authorities obviously do not share the views of Commander Denton and others as to the legal status of captured pilots. The most authoritative view I could get on the matter was from Pham Van Bach, President of the Supreme Court of the DRV and Vice-President of the Vietnam Jurists' Association. To my question as to whether the pilots were regarded as prisoners of war, he replied as follows:

"As is well-known, the US Government is waging a brazen, undeclared war of aggression in Vietnam—a war of aggression in South Vietnam and a war of destruction against the Democratic Republic of Vietnam, a sovereign and independent state, a member of the socialist camp. This was is in itself a crime, a crime against peace, a violation of the fundamental rights of the peoples, a crime against mankind. The US Government has daily launched indiscriminate air raids on hospitals, schools, and densely populated areas, resorting even to B-52's, napalm, phosphorus bombs, poison gas, toxic chemicals, etc., to massacre the Vietnamese people in a most atrocious manner and with a character of extermination. In so doing, it has most seriously violated its international pledges, the 1954 Geneva Agreements on Vietnam, the 1949 Geneva Conventions on the protection of victims of war and the norms of international law. The war crimes it is committing now in Vietnam are comparable to the crimes perpetrated in the past by the Hitlerite fascist ringleaders who have been condemned by the Nuremberg International Court.

"For this reason, the US pilots captured in North Vietnam who, carrying out the US Government's orders, have attacked our country and perpetrated numerous crimes here are air pirates; we regard them as criminals and will try them in accordance with the laws of the Democratic Republic of Vietnam."

The wave of attacks against urban centers which started in mid-April 1966, coinciding with the use of B-52's against the

North for the first time, appeared to be the application of the latest thesis at General Westmoreland's Saigon headquarters that the war in the South could only be won by "breaking the North." Throughout May the bombing of urban centers continued. On May 6, the village of Quynh Lap, to which the lepers from the hospital destroyed in June 1965 had been evacuated, was heavily bombed and strafed, 30 more lepers being killed and 34 wounded. During May and June the light industry centers of Yen Bay and Viet Tri were attacked, the escalation against the urban centers being climaxed by the raids on June 29 against the Hanoi-Haiphong fuel depots.

Repeated warnings that captured American pilots would be tried as criminals—including my interview with the President of the North Vietnam Supreme Court which was broadcast over world TV networks from early May onward—were officially ignored by the US government until after the world outcry against the Hanoi-Haiphong bombings. Perhaps to divert attention, every White House official from President Johnson down made horrified statements regarding Hanoi's declared intention to try the pilots and threatened by implication to wipe out Hanoi and Haiphong if the pilots were put on trial. The DRV was accused of violating the 1949 Geneva Convention on treatment of prisoners of war. But in this the Americans appear to be basing themselves on the principle that "might is right" and that there is one law for the rich and another for poor, one for whites and another for colored people. They are demanding that standards be applied to their prisoners very different from the barbaric treatment meted out to captured personnel of the Liberation Armed Forces in South Vietnam.

Certain of the pilots who have taken part in attacks against hospitals, schools, sanatoria and other purely civilian targets are in the hands of the North Vietnamese authorities. Scrupulously careful legal dossiers have been prepared against them. The hour and date is there, the serial number and markings of the planes, the pilots who flew them to the targets and whose hands released the bombs and fired the guns. Eye-witnesses, victims and relatives of victims are on hand to give evidence.

The North Vietnamese government takes the view that the pilots are not covered by the August 12, 1949, Geneva Convention which in its Article 2 states: "The present Convention shall apply to all cases of *declared war* or of any other armed conflict which may arise between two or more of the High Contracting parties, even *if the state of war* is not recognized by one of them." There is no *state of war* recognized by either party in this case and North Vietnam considers itself the victim of piratical air attacks, similar to those waged from the sea by the Barbary Corsairs and others of their ilk in the days of organized piracy. In South Vietnam in 1965, long after the commitment of American combat troops, the American Military Command issued a directive forbidding the use of the words "prisoners of war" in connection with their armed personnel missing in action in North or South Vietnam. Reporting this in *The New York Times* (International Edition, September 30, 1965), Saigon correspondent Neil Sheehan explained: "Because there has been no declaration of war . . . these men known to be prisoners are officially listed as 'detainees.' "

James Reston in *The New York Times,* July 13, 1966, complained about the spectacle of American pilots "being led helpless and handcuffed at gun point through menacing crowds" and praises the American people for having been "troubled but calm" up till now. He goes on to say the "rules of war specifically forbid the retribution now being discussed in the Communist world." This and similar enraged American comment seems to reveal a racist aspect. The American press in January of this year published photographs of a line of "suspected guerrillas" being marched under American guns, bound to each other with halters around their necks with slip knots, so that if one staggered or stumbled he would be strangled.

Reston should recall what *The New York Times* Saigon correspondent, Neil Sheehan, wrote on September 30, 1965, in an article entitled, "Vietnam: The Unofficial Brutality": "The United States is in the unhappy position of asking humane treatment for American prisoners of Communists while it has declined to guarantee similar treatment to Vietcong taken prisoners by American ground combat units. Such prisoners, after a preliminary interrogation, are handed over to the Vietnamese authorities by whom of course they can be and frequently are subjected to brutality. . . . The guerrillas are looked upon as rebels and traitors and a Vietcong prisoner is thus entirely at the whim of his captors. Vietnamese army police and para-military organizations such as the national guard and the militia frequently shoot Vietcong captives out of hand, beat or brutally torture them or otherwise mistreat them. . . .

"The favorite methods of torture used by Government troops are to slowly beat a captive, drag him behind a moving vehicle, apply electrodes to sensitive parts of his body or block his mouth while water spiced with hot pepper is poured down his nostrils." I could add a whole list of other revolting forms of torture perpetrated on patriots whom I have interviewed and whose bodies provided the most eloquent testimony to the veracity of their reports.

The 1949 Geneva Convention does apply specifically to the war in South Vietnam where two sides are engaged in hostilities. Article 3 (a) prohibits "violence to life and person, in particular murder of all kinds, mutilation, cruel treatment and torture." Article 4A (1) specifies that prisoners of war include "Members of the armed forces of a Party to the conflict as well as members of militias or volunteer corps forming part of such armed forces" and further provisions make it clear that they apply equally as well in a civil war as in an international conflict.

Vietnamese leaders have long believed that no legal, moral or humanitarian considerations would stay the hands of the Pentagon in further escalation. A special 11-member commission, headed by Health Minister Dr. Pham Ngoc Thach, was set up in July 1966 to collect evidence, village by village, school by school, hospital by hospital, to complete their dossiers on individual pilots and on those ultimately responsible in Washington. Hanoi endorsed the idea of Bertrand Russell to set up a War Crime's Tribunal somewhere in Western Europe and try President Johnson and other key US figures for "crimes against humanity."

If the threat to try the pilots did nothing more, it once again brought home to people all over the world the illegality of the American aggression against the Vietnamese people. It also forced the American Command in Saigon implicitly and belatedly to admit its own flagrant violations of the 1949 Geneva

Convention and all norms of civilized behavior by announcing, on July 21, 1966, that in the future prisoners of the Liberation Front's regular armed forces captured by American troops would no longer be turned over to the Saigon authorities for the sort of treatment that Sheehan has described. Guerrilla fighters and local self-defense militia, however, were not covered by the new regulations—contrary to the 1949 Geneva Convention, as the International Red Cross has repeatedly pointed out to the US Command in Saigon.

There is no doubt that if the Nuremberg standards were applied to the US pilots, a number of them could not escape the death penalty. Indiscriminate massacre of civilian population was one of the crimes that sent those convicted under the Nuremberg verdicts to the gallows.

Until an order was issued on September 24, 1965, pilots of the American Air Force and Navy were permitted to bomb and strafe at will in what were designated "free strike zones." These zones were that part of South Vietnamese territory not controlled by Saigon. Pilots returning with unused bombs and bullets could discharge them against any village they thought fit in the "free strike zones" without prior checks with their command. It meant that the civilian population of 10,000,000 in the Liberation Front areas were "legitimate" targets to be massacred at the whim of the pilots. If the Saigon forces decided to withdraw from a certain post, the villages surrounding them automatically became "free strike zones." They varied from day to day and very often the villagers had no idea that suddenly they had become "legitimate targets." On the average about 100 of such zones were listed but the number varied according to the fortunes of war. Occasionally there was an "error" so gross that it could not be hushed up, as when the pilots dumped their high explosives and napalm on villages clearly in the Saigon-controlled areas.

The directive of September 24, 1965, halting this practice as far as US planes are concerned, was probably issued because the "errors" were becoming too frequent and the stigma attached to the US Air Force and Navy had unpleasant repercussions in Saigon. However, the South Vietnamese Air Force, which also has American pilots, was free to continue the "free strike zone" attacks—another case of "looking the other way," as was done when prisoners were handed over to the Saigon forces. In explaining the new directive in *The New York Times,* October 3, 1965, correspondent R. W. Apple noted: "Many critics of U.S. policy, including some officers assigned here, have argued that air power . . . might eventually drive civilians into the Vietcong ranks."

In any case, the "free strike zone" tactic was replaced by saturation bombing of Liberation Front areas by B-52's, using an infra-red device which recorded concentrations of population by the heat given off, according to press accounts. This might well include, for instance, inhabitants of a village huddled in their air-raid shelters. The avowed aim was either to wipe out population in the Liberation Front areas or force people to leave and be concentrated in urban versions of the "strategic hamlets," camps enclosed by barbed wire at the outskirts of Saigon and other cities.

In the face of these criminal acts in Vietnam—North and South—it is ludicrous, to say the least, for American authorities responsible for such acts to condemn as "savage" or "barbarous" the idea of putting on trial some of the pilots involved.

The United States participated in drawing up the law under which the Nuremberg trials were held, in preparing the indictments, in the actual trials and in the final judgments. It is therefore doubly subject to the standards of international law established at Neuremberg. This is not the place to give a complete analysis of those historic indictments and trials, but it might be well to point out certain elements that do apply clearly to the crimes being perpetrated by US armed power against the whole of Vietnam, especially the individual responsibility for such crimes.

Article Six of the International Military Tribunal Charter, setting up the Nuremberg trials, lists among crimes "for which there shall be individual responsibility":

"(a) CRIMES AGAINST PEACE: namely, planning, preparation, initiation, or waging of war of aggression, or a *war in violation of international treaties, agreements or assurances* . . . (and) . . .

"(b) WAR CRIMES: namely, violations of the laws or customs

of war. Such violations shall include . . . plunder of public or private property, *wanton destruction of cities, towns or villages, or devastation not justified by military necessity."*

Articles Seven and Eight of the Charter state that "the official position of defendants, whether as Heads of State or responsible officials in Government Departments, shall not be considered as freeing them from responsibility or mitigating punishment" and "the fact that the Defendant acted pursuant to orders of his Government or of a superior shall not free him from responsibility." (*Nazi Conspiracy and Aggression,* U.S. Government Printing Office, Washington, D.C., 1946, Vol. I, pp. 5–6.) On pages 49–50 of the same document, the indictment of the major war criminals listed among other charges: "In Holland there was most widespread and extensive destruction, not justified by military necessity, *including the destruction of harbors, locks, dykes and bridges."* (All emphasis added.)

In view of what is going on in the South and in the North, it is indeed a tribute to the discipline and truly civilized outlook of the Vietnamese people that pilots have been humanely treated from the moment of their capture. Although, as the Vietnamese express it, there is a "heavy debt of blood to settle with the air pirates," the population seems content to let this debt be settled through the process of law. But one can hardly blame them for being embittered about the flood of pleas for "humane" treatment of the pilots usually coupled with harsh epithets and threats from world leaders most of whom have never uttered a word of reproach for this limitless air savagery, this ruthless use of US air power against a largely defenseless population, much less a word of compassion for its victims. The racist overtones of this attitude is not lost on the Vietnamese people and the people of Asia as a whole.

Chapter 4

ECONOMY FOR A LONG WAR

One day I had been passing through a village on a quest that had nothing to do with economic planning. As our little group neared the outskirts, a rhythmic, familiar clatter of machines impinged more and more on the ears. There, where the rice fields ended and clumps of bamboo and banana palms started, where water buffalo plodded along a freshly widened and paved lane, weaving looms were pounding away under an improvised shelter, a mere roof supported by poles.

Inquiry confirmed that the machines, and the fresh-faced girls tending them, accounted for part of the gaps I had photographed earlier at Hanoi's big March 8 textile mill. There I had seen empty sections of weaving and other departments, where only bolts embedded in concrete marked the spots machines had stood at, and charts of production figures with feminine names in evidence noted the labor heroines. Trucks were then being loaded with machines that cluttered the entrance to the spinning and weaving sections, while groups of women, some of them with babies, squatted around, bundles at their side, waiting to clamber aboard when the loading was finished. Other departments were still working normally at Hanoi, but in the village it was explained that part of the weaving section had been installed there and an excited young forewoman, her hair flecked with white from flying fluff, rushed out notebook in hand to inform me that production per loom was higher than in Hanoi. "We consider our looms now as machine guns against the enemy," said one of the girls as she left her loom to suckle a fat, little baby brought to a shelter opposite by a white-gowned creche attendant.

"Can an economy really work with that degree of dispersal and fragmentation?" I asked the Planning Commission expert. And I had in mind the machine tools working in a grotto; another plant actually turning out a few machine tools; part of a factory turning out electric pumps for irrigation; another making bicycle parts and bits and pieces of others I had stumbled across during my various excursions into the countryside. There were also the convoys of machinery I had seen moving along the roads in remote districts, hauling parts obviously intended for cement plants.

"Yes, it can work and it does work," he replied. "But it is not something you can find the answer to with cost accounting. First you must understand that our general line is 'All For Victory.' For this we must fight back against the US war of destruction. And we must anticipate the worst, even if the Americans escalate the war into an actual invasion of our territory. To counter that we must develop our economic base and also new techniques to meet the present war situation and all forseeable developments. Above all we must develop agricultural production, of which I will speak later.

"To reply more specifically to your question: Parallel to what we call our technical revolution, we must also make a new distribution of our productive forces. We must build up new economic bases, establish machinery in new zones suitable for the present war situation and to create conditions for victory later. Industrial development in our mountain regions is very important for our national defense, but not only for protection against bombings or invasion attempts. It is important also for the future development of the country. Together with the technical revolution and the redistribution of our economic potential we can—and the figures prove it—step up labor productivity and strengthen our economic and defense capacity. It is difficult for many of our foreign friends to understand this, but it is so.

"Another of our principles is that we must rely mainly on our own strength. Of course we appreciate, and we need, aid from our friends. But we must do everything possible ourselves. The main enemy blows must fall on our shoulders and the main blows dealt them must be dealt by our brains and muscles. We must apply the principle of 'Become Self-Supporting' on a national and regional basis. Each zone should become economically, even militarily, self-supporting, in agriculture as in industry. From the embattled fourth zone [the coastal regions leading to the 17th parallel] to the plains of the Red

River delta and in the northern and western mountain regions, all should become economically autonomous, ready to counter the enemy's attacks whenever they come, however they come and from wherever they come. You've seen only some tiny fragments of this relocation of industry. If you could see how all the parts fitted together, as we see it translated into production figures, you would have another view of things."

When I asked to have a glimpse of this overall view of things, Doan Trong Truyen provided the following data, showing the increase in production in 1965 as compared with 1964:

Overall Agricultural Production	3.3%	
Overall Industrial Production	8.4%	
Production of Industries directly under State Ministries	12.0%	
Machine-Building Industry	14.0%	
Industrial Crops	7.3%	*(acreage sown)*
" "	25.4%	*(per hectare yield)*

Overall increase in industrial production included the output of machine tools, equipment for regional industries and for transport and communications, all of which were well above the 1964 levels. Also included were output of electricity, coal, cement and even textiles, despite the bombing of the big Nam Dinh textile mill in July 1965 and the subsequent evacuation of much of its equipment. Output of local industry, including that from newly established plants, was up by 40 per cent.

"A big factor in these increases," continued Doan Trong Truyen, "was the setting up of small and medium-sized plants. We had to halt or slow down the construction of big centralized units and speed up that of the smaller ones. We are speeding them up especially in the mountain regions. Apart from wartime necessity, this is also economically sound. With the smaller units we get production and returns on investment much sooner."

Did not all this play havoc with economic planning? What happened to the industrialization program? What happened to orders placed in the socialist countries for equipment of big, centralized plants?

"Our first five-year industrialization plan covered the 1961–65 period," answered the planning expert. "It was primarily aimed at building the material and technical basis for socialism. It was going very well and by 1964 we were working out the main lines of a second five-year plan. The first American attacks in August 1964, and the systematic air raids that started in February 1965, forced us to change our plans, but not our aims. Till then, economic construction was our main task, with attention also to national defense needs. Harmonizing the requirements of each was one of our problems. Since the American attacks we had to change the emphasis. Our main task now is to mobilize all the nation's human, material and financial resources to intensify production, above all to satisfy our own defense needs in the North. We consider the South as the great front-line area for the whole country and the North as the great rear area for the whole country.

"We had to scrap our ideas for a new five-year plan and draw up a stop-gap two-year plan based primarily on war needs but continuing at the same time the general line of building the technical and material base for socialism. We will not permit the war to apply brakes to our economic development. Instead it will give, and is giving, new impetus to our productive forces. As for the question of orders placed in the socialist countries, we sent a delegation headed by our Vice-Premier to the socialist countries to explain our changed requirements. We had to cancel orders for all sorts of plant equipment and replace them with orders for smaller units, suitable for our dispersal of industry and our program to build up many small units instead of big centralized ones."

"What comes after the two-year plan?"

"That depends on the course of the war. We think we have to take into account that the war may last ten or 20 years or more and we plan the training of technical cadres, for instance, on that basis. But should victory come sooner, our planning could quickly be adjusted accordingly. The two-year plan is a sort of transition plan which can be continued to expand wartime industry or switched to peacetime development. As for agriculture, the tasks remain the same—to continue to apply new techniques to expand to the utmost agricultural production. We are engaged in what we call a 'technical revolution' in the countryside."

"What about agriculture?" I asked. "Where is all your manpower coming from, if not from the peasantry? How can you squeeze the maximum out of the land and at the same time drain the countryside of its manpower? One sees practically only women on the land these days. Not just planting rice seedlings as in the past, but doing the ploughing and other field work?"

"It is true," Doan Trong Truyen agreed, "the women have largely taken over in the countryside. There is a labor shortage on the land. But don't forget that until recently surplus manpower was the main problem in the countryside."

This was also true. The last time I had investigated the problem, in 1962, I found that with only one-eleventh of a hectare (about 900 square yards) of arable land per head of population, peasants in the rice-growing cooperatives were having difficulty in squeezing out more than 100 work-days in many parts. There were obvious limits to what each co-op member could do when they were so thick on the land. There was obviously no great interest in mechanization which would cut back still further the yearly work-days, on which earnings were based, in a country where industrialization moved far too slowly to provide alternative employment.

"It is the labor shortage caused by the war that provides the impetus for the technical revolution in the countryside," continued Doan Trong Truyen, "even though this is still very modest by western standards," he conceded. "1965 was the first year of some low-level mechanization in the co-ops and the fifth-month harvest was our first wartime crop.* We met with great difficulties in February and March, especially in the coastal areas where the bombers were overhead all the time. Climatic conditions were also unfavorable. But the harvest was a record, the biggest ever for area planted and per hectare yield.

"For the tenth-month crop, there were many more difficulties— floods, drought and insects, not to mention bombs and a reduced

* In North Vietnam there are two main rice crops yearly. That sown in the winter and reaped in the fifth lunar month; that sown in the late spring and reaped in the tenth lunar month. They are referred to as the fifth- and tenth-month harvests, respectively.

labor force. But the yields were still good, not as good as the fifth month, but good enough to make the year as a whole the best of our five-year plan. It was in the heavily bombed coastal areas, and in the heaviest bombed provinces in that area, that the harvest was best. The coastal areas were 14 per cent up over the previous year. Apart from the high morale, stepped up by the bombings, the increased yield was due to better irrigation with lots of new electric pumps installed; intensified use of fertilizers; better seed selection—application in fact of some elements of our 'technical revolution.' Some 700 of our 28,000 cooperatives reached five tons of rice per hectare, thus demonstrating the real possibility of attaining this everywhere. The average production in 1939, the record prewar year, was 1.5 to 1.6 tons per hectare with up to three tons in the rare cases where two crops were planted. But two crops a year were the exception in those days, whereas it is the rule now with 80 per cent of our cooperatives."

"What does the 1965 crop represent in terms of your food needs?" I asked.

"It means that we were able to continue stocking rice on a far greater scale than ever before," Truyen replied. "The total put into stock in 1965 greatly surpassed that of previous years. Mainly this was due to the good harvest but partly also to the patriotism of the peasants who kept less back for themselves. We were able to put 23 per cent of the total harvest into our reserves and we encouraged the cooperatives to create reserves of their own as well. Provided there are no great natural disasters, it means we can attain real self-sufficiency in foodstuffs. The various zones and provinces can become self-sufficient as well. This removes a big burden from our transport system and a big headache from those who used to have to worry about food distribution in case interprovincial communications are really badly damaged. On the agricultural front, one can say it was a very encouraging first year of war."

"Is there not the usual wartime tendency of hoarding and spiraling food prices? Don't socialist principles tend to be thrown overboard in such a situation? How do you acquire rice for the reserves?"

"We started stocking rice a few years ago," Truyen continued.

"The cooperatives are obliged to sell the state fixed amounts of grain at fixed prices over a set period of time—five years, for instance. The state pays 33 sau per kilogram for unhusked paddy and this is retailed to the consumer at 40 sau.* But in order to stimulate production and avoid the peasants having to sell their surpluses on the free market, in 1965 we paid a 50-per-cent bonus for grain delivered above the quota. On the other hand, to promote socialist principles, we encouraged 'mutual aid' among co-op members. That is, if anyone was temporarily short of grain, other co-op members should supply it at the same fixed prices as paid by the state so that there should be no exploitation of misfortune. In this way the laws of socialism would be applied and the people's traditions of humanism and patriotism developed. This has worked well.

"There has been some slight rise in prices on the free market. In the year starting February 1965, some food prices—mainly vegetables, eggs and fish—rose an average of 25 to 27 per cent on the free market. Despite this, one can say that prices remained stable because 85 per cent of all foodstuffs are purchased through State enterprises where prices have remained fixed. There is no hoarding because wholesale trade is between the co-operatives and the state purchasing organizations, and the State controls almost all the retail trade. Individual hoarding is almost unknown because of the fundamental unity and patriotism of our people and their confidence in the government."

By my own checks in Hanoi and village markets and among consumers, I found the price rises were as he said. But rice was being sold in some village free markets at 80 sau a kilogram, twice the official price. Rationing of rice, pork and sugar had been introduced since 1957 and no new items had been added to the ration lists nor had there been any reduction in rations because of the war. Most families assured me that the ration of 13 kilograms of rice per adult and ten kilograms per child was sufficient, and it was rare that they had to buy on the free market. Wheat bread, which is on sale at all town and village markets, is non-rationed. There was an abundance of vegetables, meat, fish and fruit in all the Hanoi markets and roadside mar-

* 100 sau = 1 dong, the DRV monetary unit; 3.5 dong = $1 (US).

kets in the countryside. Prices for many consumer goods were substantially lower than they had been two years previously.

"In 1964," explained Doan Trong Truyen, "decisions were taken at the highest level on the question of trade and prices. The main point was to stabilize prices, adjust those that were unreasonable and push for a general reduction. Then came the war. How could the policy be applied? Many of our experts thought this policy must be shelved. Our leaders opposed this. We have to carry on the war, they argued, but we also have to push ahead with building socialism. Prices are an important element in the latter so we must stick to the policy of price stabilization and reduction. During the past 12 months important reductions [30 to 60 per cent, as I found by checks in the shops] have been made in such items as paper, text books, medicine, bicycles, radios, textiles for clothing and others. This is almost unprecedented in wartime," Truyen said with justifiable pride. "That we could do this is due to our experience during the first resistance, to state control over production and distribution and to the confidence the people have in the administration. We are now pushing ahead with price reductions for machines in industry and agriculture, in timber and coal supplied to the cooperatives. We also intend to lower systematically the prices of means of production. We must never for a moment lose sight of the fact that we are building socialism."

"Socialism includes constantly rising living standards," I said. "With the great mobilization of manpower, the economic and social upheaval connected with the relocation of industries and the labor force, and the evacuation of the cities, living standards will inevitably fall. Will this not be a backward step as far as building socialism is concerned?"

"We won't be able to improve living standards for quite a while," he replied. "But we will try and maintain them at their present level. We frankly ask the people to accept privations in a spirit of self-sacrifice and patriotism, to accept austerity and practice strict economy. We seek to assure that minimum vital needs are met—rice, sugar, salt, kerosene, textiles—all at reasonable, fixed prices; not only through the shops where unequal distribution may occur if only those with ready cash have access.

Where shortages occur—needles, matches or cigarettes, for instance in some areas—we deliver them in sufficient quantities direct to the cooperatives or factories for distribution through cooperative or trade union channels. In that way we insure that those who most need the goods will get them and any possibility of price increase or hoarding is eliminated. We don't think that socialist principles suffer because of this. On the contrary; everyone sees that the burdens and sacrifices are shared as equally as possible and also what benefits we can make available."

"With the wholesale mobilization of manpower, especially the youth, is there not a danger to the higher educational system you have built up in recent years? Are you not gambling with your future in drafting thousands of students and future technical cadres into the armed forces and construction projects?"

"For a complete answer to that," replied Truyen, "you had better talk with the Ministry of Education, I can answer only in part. True, we have mobilized tens and hundreds of thousands of young people. Almost all our youth, over three million of them, have enrolled in the 'three-readies' movement.* We mobilized 250,000 for the mountain regions alone, to help build up the new economy in the backward areas. We mobilized many more tens of thousands to build the new communications networks and help repair bomb damage. But we have not touched the 90,000 students who are being trained as specialists, technical cadres and skilled workers. Nor have we touched their teachers. They are our precious capital for the future. For the tasks of war if it lasts that long, but above all for the grandiose tasks of peace afterwards."

An example of the dispersal of industry and the efforts to make each province as economically autonomous as possible is to be found in Quang Binh province, which borders along the 17th parallel and has taken the brunt of the bombings. During 1965 and early 1966 a network of machine shops was set up in

* The "three readies" are (1) Ready to fight and fight valiantly, ready to enlist in the armed forces; (2) ready to overcome all difficulties, to stimulate production work and studies, under any circumstances whatsoever, and (3) ready to go anywhere and perform any task required by the Motherland.

every district, as well as shops at province level, to manufacture and repair a wide range of equipment for industry, agriculture and transport. These include small rice threshing, husking and winnowing machines; hand carts to replace the traditional shoulder poles and baskets; ploughshares and harrows, hoes, spades, etc.; primitive types of ball bearings and presses for bricks and tiles. Small plants were also set up to manufacture cement, insecticides and fertilizers and a whole range of essential consumer goods, matches, cigarettes, soap, sugar, crockery, paper and other items. All of this was new to the province, the small plants and workshops blossoming into life literally under storms of bombs and bullets. The resultant saving in transport was considerable, and shortages that would otherwise have been inevitable, with Quang Binh at the very end of the long haul from Hanoi, were avoided.

Investment in such regional industries was doubled in 1966 as compared to the previous year. State shops and the local markets wherever I traveled displayed an impressive variety of articles from the newly established plants. Many started as handicraft cooperatives but quickly expanded into compact little industries, as skills were acquired and machines made available. Priority was given to industries which serviced transport or turned out a wide variety of carts—drawn by hand or animal or bicycle-powered, as well as trailers for trucks and the like.

Another impressive aspect was the multitude of small electric-power generators all over the country, on the plains as well as in the mountain areas, some powered by locally produced coal, others by liquid fuel, the latter stored in deep underground shelters. It was also interesting that the 1966–67 plan provided for a considerable stepping up of mineral prospecting and for further vast irrigation and flood-prevention projects, air attacks against dikes and dams having become a commonplace by early 1966.

In general, the 1966–67 plan, on top of what had already been accomplished in 1965, was the most concrete evidence that North Vietnam had switched over to a long-war economy.

Chapter 5

LEARNING UNDER BOMBS

It is a fairly common sight in the coastal areas at night to see from afar lines of tiny glow worms wriggling along the roads and paths. As one approaches, the glow worms turn into children, tiny kerosene lamps in hand and school books tucked under their arms. If you meet them by day, their backs are well covered with palm fronds and other greenery, ready to hurl themselves face down between rows of potatoes or maize, or jump into the nearest holes, if planes come. Learning must go on at all levels even under bombs; it is one of the laws of the land.

"How to carry on after 170 primary and secondary schools and educational institutes were bombed to bits and hundreds of pupils and teachers killed? After virtually all our schools in the countryside had to be abandoned and most of the children in our cities evacuated?" It was the question put to me by Education Minister, Nguyen Van Huyen, normally a placid, calm man but obviously agitated by the magnitude of his problems. "And with 2,900,000 pupils doing general education, we have 300,000 more than last year. Can you imagine what that means in terms of protection, classrooms, teachers?"

"How are you managing?" was the obvious question.

"We managed by transferring all our first-cycle schools* to the agricultural cooperatives. Before they were at village level.† In that way the children don't have to move around so much, classrooms are a few hundred yards away. We can keep the smallest children off the roads altogether. Second-cycle schools till now were in the district centers; now they are at village

* General education in North Vietnam is divided into three cycles: first to fourth class; fifth to seventh class, and eighth to tenth.
† Every Vietnamese village comprises three to five hamlets. The agricultural cooperatives are now organized at hamlet level, except in a few very rare cases, as at Xuan Thanh (see Chapter 1, p. 20) where they are organized at village level. A North Vietnamese hamlet in general comprises 200 to 400 households.

level. Like the first-cycle schools it meant breaking them up into smaller units. Now every village in many of the provinces has its second-cycle school. In the third-cycle schools, the children are older, can fend better for themselves, but they have also been brought down from provincial level to one for every district. We have done everything possible to bring the schools close to the pupils, close to their families. We have absolutely abandoned multi-story buildings and every classroom has subterranean communication trenches starting right at the desks, leading out to deep shelters in the open fields or some place away from the buildings. It is because the parents have confidence in the measures we have taken for protection, that our school population has increased this year."

It was fairly clear that the magnitude of Minister Nguyen Van Huyen's problems and the organizational measures taken to meet them, provided the answer as to whether schools and other non-military targets were really being attacked or not. To change from one day to another the educational regime of nearly three million children must have been a major headache—not only for the Minister.

"What were your major difficulties?"

"There were three," he replied. "First, buildings. We had to walk out of all the multi-story, brick buildings we had built since the end of the war against the French. We can't build new ones, not even in bamboo except under very special circumstances. We don't want to change the physiognomy of the countryside—new buildings will bring new bombs. Here and there we can build classrooms under trees, where they will look like peasants' huts, but we cannot build complexes of buildings, or big structures even in bamboo, since the Americans will wipe them out as they did the brick ones. This is our biggest single problem."

"How then are you solving the problem of classrooms?"

"We had to count on help from the parents, asking them to put their homes at our disposal. Families crowd into the kitchen during part of the day or night to put the rest of the house at our disposal. Sometimes two families combine together in a single house or three families in two houses and the other is at our disposal. It's a matter of patriotism and national pride among parents that the bombers shall not halt their children learning. Where we build, it is on the basis of single classrooms. In the poorer, smaller hamlets we usually have to build one or two classrooms.

"Buildings, that's the biggest problem. But running a close second is that of teachers. Smaller classes means more teachers. In a very short time we had to double the number of teachers in certain categories; first- and second-cycle classes averaged 40 to 50 pupils each, now they are 20 to 25. How did we cope? After the campaign to wipe out illiteracy was completed in 1958, we opened complementary courses in general education for those who were outside school age. That is adult education at evening or other spare-time courses. Teachers of these complementary courses were a source to draw on. In all villages now there are young people who have completed seven years of general education. They now work in the cooperatives. That was another source. With these as our raw material for first- and second-cycle schools, in six months we trained many thousands of new teachers. But still for all of North Vietnam, we are short 13,000 teachers. Apart from the systematically bombed areas where teaching goes on at night, we have switched to two classes a day. In 10,000 evacuated schools one teacher does the work of two, one class in the morning, another in the afternoon.

"The third major problem is the evacuated school. The bombing of the Huong Phoc school in Ha Tinh province on February 9 this year was a serious warning to us; 33 pupils were killed and 24 injured. After that we speeded up the evacuation of schools from the towns. Despite our efforts at construction over the past ten years we've not been able to do much building of homes, or improve amenities very much. Living standards improved, but there are not many new homes in the villages. We built plenty of factories, institutes and schools, but alongside these, even outside Hanoi, peasant huts still remain without electric light or running water. So there was no point in evacuating children to villages on the outskirts of the cities. We decided to ask parents to send them back to their native villages—almost every city dweller has his native village, with relatives still on the land—and let the town children be integrated in existing, local classes without trying to create special classes for them.

In cases where the evacuees would be a material burden our local organs would help.

"By and large, evacuation was handled in that way, especially for children in the first- and second-cycle schools. There are exceptions. Children of personnel working in the public service, various ministries, etc., can be grouped together in special boarding schools, which can be financed by the administration concerned. And third-cycle schools, where the children are older and can look after themselves, can be evacuated to a village, where they can set up their own kitchen, do their own cooking and become more or less autonomous. The pupils can do a certain amount of work at the cooperatives or some state enterprises, earn some money and contribute something to their upkeep. We will provide the rest."

Minister Huyen went on to explain that evacuation, splitting up families, involved much more than strains on the sentiments. It imposed material difficulties. Budgeting for two or three separate units, even for food, was more expensive. Families are used to sharing such things as beds, mosquito nets, blankets and thermos flasks among several children. The Ministry had "to keep an eye on such things and see that all lived adequately." To an outsider, I must say, it all seemed to have worked very smoothly. I spent a good deal of time in the villages and cooperatives, visiting many of the peasant-hut classrooms and schools where town children had been integrated, and talked to Hanoi families whose children were evacuated. It seemed to me things went very well, and I said so. "Don't expect our people to pour out their griefs to a foreigner," said Minister Huyen when I spoke of my impressions. "We know their difficulties, but we try and prevent them from getting out of hand. Our government does what it can."

I had met mothers in Hanoi who visited their children once or twice a month and were very pleased with their physical condition and especially by the way they had quickly adapted themselves psychologically to village life. "Many, many city children all over the world dream of living in the countryside and looking after cows and chickens," said Nguyen Van Huyen, "and it's the same in Vietnam. We have a problem of intensifying production on the land with reduced manpower. Our schools must take part also. If we keep within our school walls some three million children as non-producers then this would be a hindrance to the war. In any case, it would be against a basic principle of our education system—to link schools with life, education with production. With the evacuation of tens of thousands of city children and teachers—and our pressing war problems—plus having established schools in the agricultural cooperatives, there are excellent conditions for pupils and teachers to take part in production. Each school now has its plan of aid to the co-ops—how much manure will be delivered, how many days of digging irrigation trenches. Even children of eight and nine can look after buffalo and ducks, and they love it.

"There are plans and norms and children get paid, according to work points, just as co-op members. Some children earn as much as full members. From the town they bring new techniques, especially in thinking up gadgets to avoid the most backbreaking work. Any number of children of 13 or 14 years have not only succeeded in supporting themselves financially but support one or two other members of their family. In this way they feel they are aiding the war effort. But teachers have the strictest instructions to insure that work shall in no way interfere with studies."

I asked if this tremendous upheaval in the life of pupils and teachers, the fact that thousands of new teachers had to be trained in six months and that in many cases they often had to take two classes a day and double their teaching hours, would not lead to a drastic lowering of standards.

"Yes and no," replied Minister Huyen. "It's obvious that you can't study the same under bombs as you can without them. We have to count with intensified bombardments, down to village level. We may have to reduce teaching time. We have to select a study program that takes this into account and even count on omitting part of the program. In this case we will urge our teachers to teach exceptionally well and our pupils to learn exceptionally well that part which remains. We will have to make a careful choice, in that case. That choice must be dictated by our national reality. We will concentrate, for instance, on our own national language and how to handle it properly. Also on the natural sciences and math. History and geography may be reduced a little; the children can make that up through literature later. We will need technical cadres, strong in physics, chemistry, mathematics, biology.

"We also have to differentiate between our geographic zones and select programs accordingly. In Vinh Linh and Quang Binh (both just north of the 17th parallel) where bombardments are very intensive, we must have a special program but we must also be flexible so as to switch the program according to the degree and geographic direction of escalation. But everything, even with cuts, modifications and switches of program, is aimed at pushing ahead with the revolution. 'Teach well, study well' is the national slogan for education and we will see to it that quality of what is taught will be maintained, and improved. In fact the whole educational system is to be improved, starting right now."

"Improved?"

Minister Huyen went on to explain that in order to meet my request for an interview he had left a nation-wide conference of education experts, including all department chiefs of his ministry and provincial education officers, at which the finishing touches were being given to a breath-taking new deal for education.

"Although our urgent national task is to win the war," he explained, "our leaders also have their eyes on the future. There is an urgent need to train technical cadres. To do that we need teachers. It's a long-term project. In three years we must train teachers in order to get technical cadres five years after that. But we have to start sometime—and it has been decided that we start right now. Until recently we have taken in 800 to 1,000 trainees for secondary school teachers. But for the 1966–67 school year we will take in 2,500. And during the past few years there have been an average of 15,000 students who matriculated. That will be the figure for this school year. But our aim in five to six years' time is 40,000. We need the figure of 40,000 to prepare technical cadres for the South as well as the North. After the war, we want to take 'giant steps' and we'll need cadres able to push the country ahead at 'cosmic speed'—with technical and scientific cadres of university entrance standard. We must develop despite the war. No matter at what cost, we must train teachers so we can also make up after the war any short-comings in our education during the war. And if the war continues that long, these cadres will play a vital role in our war needs. We have to control the situation, never retreat before the American attacks.

"We have some experience in improving education under war conditions. In the first resistance war (against the French) we increased the number of teachers from 5,000 to 12,000; now we have 77,000 for general education and 90,000 if we include those teaching in complementary education. It's true also that we have never faced a war of destruction of the type the Americans are waging here, but we are confident that we can carry on. There are other aspects of the 'new deal' in education that it would be better for you to discuss at the Pedagogic Institute."

I asked if there was any modification of the program of studies because of the war.

Minister Huyen laughed and said: "Despite the war, would be a better way to put it. There are changes. We are going over to the 11-year school system, making the second-cycle four years instead of three as at present. Attendance at first-cycle schools will be compulsory and we plan that 80 per cent of pupils finishing the first-cycle will go on to the second. Emphasis in the new program is on modernity and bringing studies strictly in line with our national realities. We have to train children in the direction of the modern sciences, as is being done in France, the USA and other countries. We carefully watch what is going on there. Despite our backward situation, we must do this if we are to make the 'leap ahead' that our leaders want and the country needs. As for national reality, studies must take into account the nature and climate or our country, our soil and sub-soil, our natural resources, and our traditions. In this way we can follow the aims of our national revolution.

"By and large, the new program has been worked out. It is being tried out experimentally in certain classes and schools this year, and after modifications will be tried out on a larger scale in the 1966–67 school year. Based on the results we will go ahead with printing the new text books. We are already training teachers for the new program and one of the aims of the present conference is to make the details known to those responsible for its application."

"Could you give some examples of changes in the program?"

"Mathematics will be taught even in first-cycle schools, with a new method of teaching. Above all, in the third-cycle schools there will be lots of new, up-to-date theoretical work, modified according to new advances in science. We will be paying attention to such matters as algebraic structures. In biology, for instance, studies will be based largely on the theories of molecular biology."

"Will not the country's manpower needs, especially if the Americans continue their escalation, start swallowing up many of your teachers and university students?"

"Definitely no," he replied. "The country needs manpower for the war, but it needs cadres for the future more. We are rich enough to provide both. For instance, the numbers of our students to be sent abroad will be greatly increased. In many cases it's the only way for them to acquire technology and advanced scientific concepts. Not only will we retain and expand our present stock of teachers and students but we will draw in more university students from the non-scholastic world. We will intensify the complementary courses so that 30 per cent of our matriculated graduates will be from these adult courses. We expect to have at least one million following complementary study courses in the new school year, and the modified program will also be taught in these courses. We will follow our young people wherever they go, in the army, on the big construction jobs, so that wherever they are, they can continue their education. We did this before with the Army in peacetime; now in wartime, we must make even greater efforts. In the Army we have stepped up the general educational level from first and second year standards to an average of sixth and seventh year— very important when it comes to mastering complicated weapons and techniques," concluded Minister Nguyen Van Huyen.

At the Pedagogic Institute, there were more details on the "new deal" for education. The director of the Institute, Pham Huy Thong, a small, scholarly historian, with the thick-lensed glasses typical of many intellectuals of his generation, had also come straight from the nationwide conference on education.

He was able to tell me of decisions that even the public would not know about for several months. They were being applied immediately, even before they had gone through the process of formal approval at various levels. (One of the by-products of war, one noted, was that in North Vietnam, at least, it slashed red tape by the hundreds of miles.)

"Most important decisions have been taken," said director Thong, "because our leaders now attach the utmost importance to training teachers and technical cadres. All students in the future will receive 100-per cent financial support from the state. We have around 4,000 at our institute. New important material support will be given to teachers also."

He went on to explain that until then, only third-cycle teachers were fully paid by the state, second-cycle teachers were paid half by the state and half by the population where they taught, and first-cycle teachers received only one quarter of their salary from the state, the rest from the population. The latter always paid up, because they attached such importance to having their children well educated, but payments were irregular, depending on when the harvests had been brought in and sold. In the future, second-cycle teachers will be wholly paid by the state, which will make it easier for the local population to pay the first-cycle ones on time, and the state will insure that the latter get the same social benefits, pensions and so on, as their colleagues.

"All this represents a great stimulus to teachers and students to carry on," said Pham Huy Thong. "But we had other problems to cope with. All our young people have enlisted in the 'three readies,' many of the teachers, too. They all want to take off with a gun in their hand and shoot at Americans. We had to carry out a very serious political and ideological campaign, and enlist the help of the party and government to persuade them that studying was the best contribution they could make to beating the enemy—now and in the future."

About three-quarters of the students and professors were already evacuated to the countryside, and others were moving out even while our interview was proceeding. A strictly limited number were permitted to stay, because certain laboratory equipment in the physics and chemistry section, needing constant attention and strictly maintained temperatures, had been shifted down into deep basements, and classes which used this equipment would remain.

"The students went out into the forests, full of enthusiasm," said Mr. Thong. "They downed trees and bamboo, sawed up the timber and built new classrooms and living quarters. Within a few weeks studies started again and morale and application to work was higher than it had ever been. In fact we had two evacuations. Once, into a remote mountain area, where we decided after a while that supply and communications problems for an organization like ours were too great. We left the buildings for others for whom such problems were not so important and built again in the plains, in an area where we could grow most of our own food and be in close contact with the population. Staff and students work together to grow vegetables, raise chickens and pigs and so on." He repeated the general lines of Nguyen Van Huyen's explanation of the new program and when I asked to what extent the Institute's program had been affected by the war, he said:

"Not much. Students are taught the elements of first aid so they can be of immediate use in bombardments. First aid is now incorporated as a regular subject. We retain half those who graduate as third-cycle teachers and give them six weeks' military training, theoretical and practical, so that if they are eventually called up they'll have some notions of what to do. All students get two weeks' military training a year. A few teachers and senior students were called up in the very first days of the attacks, but this was immediately stopped. The study of physics and biology has been slightly modified by the war situation, not much."

Mr. Thong considered that one of the main by-products of the evacuation was the new relationship between teachers and students on the one hand and between the institute community as a whole and the population, on the other. "It's a two way process," he said. "Our people take an enthusiastic part in the health drive. They want decent WC's, pure water supplies and bath-houses, not only because they are used to such facilities but it is part of the national health campaign. They bring new techniques to bear and help as spare-time teachers in general education classes. But they also become integrated with the people, study their problems, enter into their lives. This is precisely one of the aims of our education. We want to train real militants, capable of carrying out what we call the 'technical revolution' and having a realistic attitude to life's problems. The war has given a great impetus to this; it is no longer theoretical or abstract.

"Our main task is to turn out third-cycle teachers. Every district now has a third-cycle school. We want teachers who stand shoulder to shoulder with the students and we want the students who become teachers to feel they are really part of the country. At the district to which they are assigned, they should not only be there as teachers, but apply their knowledge to practical affairs; taking part, for example, in the campaign to harvest five tons of rice per hectare. The tasks of the peasantry should also become, in part, their tasks. We always aimed at turning out all-rounders, but the Americans have now forced us to speed up the process."

He took me for a stroll around the Institute buildings and here, as on many other occasions, one noted that what was a great disadvantage in peacetime years was proving advantageous in the new situation. Classrooms and dormitories are poverty-stricken affairs, astonishing to find in any capital city. They are for the main part nothing more than extended peasant huts—single-storied buildings, walls of pleated bamboo and thatch roofs, the barest covers for the comfortless bare benches and desks inside the classrooms, hard bamboo and wooden beds in the dormitories.

"We started to build a few three-story brick buildings," said Pham Huy Thong almost apologetically, waving his hand to the few modern buildings on the campus, "and we intended to continue, but with the war we have had to postpone that." How much more difficult it would have been for students to have had to move out of modern glass and chrome buildings and abandon feather beds and flush toilets for the countryside! The fact that the North Vietnamese continued their austere, frugal hard-working lives, with no great differences in living conditions for workers, civil servants or intellectuals, and no great difference between town and countryside, makes the move back to the countryside far smoother than would be possible in any modern, western society, or indeed any sophisticated Asian society. It is another of those built-in defenses which the Pentagon computers are incapable of absorbing into their cipher-stream.

Pham Huy Thong was worried that teachers' training courses had been of two or three years' duration only, instead of the four or five years he considered necessary to turn out a really qualified all-rounder, with a broad general culture and an expert knowledge of his own specialty. "Although the courses are short," he said, "they are very concentrated. Demands were so great, that we could not have longer ones. Also it is difficult to retain the students. They want to jump into activity. And this is good because we need militants who are burning to get to work, but we also need them highly qualified. They have to be able to train cadres capable of working with machines appropriate to the technical requirements of our country. So we have a program of calling them back for refresher courses, maybe for one year, then back to work for a year and after that another year of studies. In the sciences, from now on, we will probably try and retain students for the full four to five years. The best of the graduates, in any case, we will keep on as professors or research students. Those who have domestic or other difficulties in taking the refresher courses, will continue to study by correspondence."

After the interview was finished, Pham Huy Thong, a small, eager figure, knapsack and rifle on his back, clambered aboard a truck with a few similarly accoutered students and started off for somewhere in the countryside where the conference on education was continuing. Despite his thick-lensed spectacles, he was also a member of the Institute's self-defense corps.

I also visited Hanoi's beautiful new Polytechnic Institute, the building and equipment a gift from the Soviet Union, a lovely, gleaming glass and concrete building with machine-gun emplacements, like storks' nests, scattered over the roofs. It is Hanoi's finest and most modern building, but marked down for abandonment even before the official opening ceremony. Useless to repeat the conversation there. The same aims, the same problems, the same dedication as at the Pedagogic Institute and as set out at the Ministry of Education. I had already stumbled across one of the evacuated faculties, metallurgical, in the jungle and was assured by the professors that since evacuation there was an all-round improvement of the scholastic level, as expressed in exam results. "They all feel the school is their own now," said one of the professors, "and after all they built it."

At what was left in the Hanoi building I was interested in one of the problems that the fourth-year Construction Faculty was engaged in. It was students of this faculty, incidentally, that manned the machine guns on the roof, under the expert eye of a regular army officer who had taken part in downing 12 planes. In one of the research laboratories, students were poring over what looked like a structure of tubular aluminum elements similar to those used as the framework of campers' tents. Only they turned out to be tubular steel, and the shape was a bit different. The structure proved to be a miniature model of what could be standardized, pre-fab sections for evacuated factory buildings. Light and mobile, the elements could easily be transported in trucks, quickly assembled and dismounted in case the vagaries of escalation made relocation again necessary.

"Our practical work is now very much geared to war needs," the professor escorting me explained, as he showed me the various instruments for testing stresses and tensions of tubular steel, the strength of welded joints, and so on. "Our practical work here has always been geared to actual production problems. Factories and engineers send us all sorts of problems to solve. Now anything to do with the war effort has absolute priority. We are still experimenting with light structural elements suitable for housing the plants which have been evacuated. The present bamboo and thatch buildings are all right as emergency structures but we must think of replacing them with something more permanent to protect valuable machinery from the worst that man and nature can do. And we have to think of something for the evacuated workers a bit more solid and comfortable than the huts and barracks they're living in now. It's not much good talking about the technical revolution if our technique can't quickly solve such problems."

As to whether the student body had been affected by the

country's manpower needs, the answer was: "We have at present 8,500 students and this year we will be taking on 50 per cent more than our normal annual intake. When we started here we had 50 teachers, now we have over 1,000; none have been mobilized, though all would go to the front if they were encouraged to do so."

That about closed my investigations as to how the war had affected the educational system, although wherever I visited in the countryside I made a point of dropping in on local schools, always finding that things worked about the way the education minister had explained.

Back at the hotel, after the visit to the Polytechnic Institute, a colleague, who had come with the friendliest intentions to support the Vietnamese people with his typewriter, was slumped over a table, his head in his hands, unhappy and troubled. "I've come to write about their sufferings," he groaned, "but all they will talk about is 'Victory'."

Chapter 6

MEDICINE OLD AND NEW

How does a backward country like Vietnam face up to the medical and surgical problems imposed by half a million or so tons of bombs a year? And the constant threats of "worse to come?"

Health Minister Dr. Pham Ngoc Thach was the obvious person to turn to for the answer. Dr. Thach, a small, stocky man, with a bronzed face and balding head and fairly radiating his inexhaustible energy, originates from the imperial family of Annam. A cousin of former Emperor Bao Dai, he threw in his lot with the Vietminh revolutionaries at an early age. After the August 1945 uprising, Pham Ngoc Thach headed the Vietminh administration set up in the Nam-Bo (Cochin-China), and when the resistance war started against the French, he left for the jungle to organize a medical service which he continued to direct and expand, setting up pharmaceutical plants in the jungle, until the war ended. (A cousin, Dr. Ho Thu, performs a similar service in the Liberation Front zones of South Vietnam today.)

A brilliant medical scientist, Dr. Thach is known among his western colleagues for his original research work on TB. He is the architect of Vietnam's health services today, having built them up brick by brick mainly from the medical schools he established in the jungle during the resistance, but also reinforced by a number of brilliant French-trained Vietnamese doctors and surgeons who gave up their often lucrative practices in Paris to serve their own people. Because the hard resistance years forced Dr. Thach to rely largely on medicinal plants and traditional medicine, he is an ardent advocate of a harmonious development of both traditional and western medicine. It is almost useless to try and find him in his ministry and the likeliest place of all is in the Hanoi TB hospital and research center. To my first and main question, he replied as follows:

"The American attacks did not catch us by surprise. Thanks to our medical organization, which goes all the way down to the agricultural cooperatives, wounded have been treated on time, and almost on the spot. In fact, all the villages in the plains have medical and maternity clinics and almost all the cooperatives have a public health organization. Seventy per cent of the villages in the highlands (where the tribal minorities live) also have their medical and maternity clinics. In peacetime, these organizations take care of the public health campaigns, vaccinations against smallpox, cholera, paratyphoid, diphtheria, tetanus, whooping cough and poliomylitis. They render first aid to the sick and send urgent surgical or obstetrical cases to their district hospital. Over 90 per cent of mothers give birth in the village maternity clinics.

"Our medical service, in other words, is solidly established at village level. So it's natural in wartime that these clinics give first aid to the wounded and treat shock cases on the spot while waiting to evacuate patients to the district hospital. For months past, in view of the savage and indiscriminate American bombings, the district surgeons often operate in the village clinics, avoiding what, after a bombing raid, are often difficult transport conditions for the patient."

"Can you have sufficient stocks of plasma or blood widely dispersed enough to treat shock and loss of blood immediately, in view of the fairly haphazard nature of the bombings?" I asked.

In answer, Dr. Thach invited me to accompany him to an improvised "operating theater" in the basement of one of the hospital buildings. On a table, two dogs lay on their sides, facing each other. A tube, through which blood was pulsing, led from one to the other, heartbeats, blood pressure and respiration automatically recorded by needles on slowly-revolving graphs. "We are still trying to discover exactly what happens to the nervous system in the case of shock of varying degrees," explained Dr. Thach. "In this experiment one of the dogs is getting blood supply fed to the brain through direct transfusion from the other, while the rest of the system is severed. This is a theoretical study." We passed into another laboratory, where a third dog was tied down to the "operating table," and as we watched half the blood was drained out of the body, flickering needles recording what was very close to death—one of the conditions of extreme shock due to loss of blood. The dog's eyes closed and he seemed perfectly inert. Nurses then gave a large intravenous injection and at the same time a solution was slowly fed in through a tube in the dog's mouth. Within seconds, the recording needles, which had started to draw the straight line of clinical death, started flickering again and soon were describing definite rythmic zig-zags as the heart and respiratory system started to work again. Within seconds the dog's eyes had opened and his body was pulsing away fairly normally.

"That's the practical application of what we have learned from our theoretical studies," Dr. Thach explained. "It is difficult for us to have stocks of plasma available everywhere for immediate emergency use. And at village level it is not always possible to make transfusions. But we have developed this method of intravenous injections of a solution that we call NTG, combined with an isotonic solution of a glucose type of serum administered orally. With this method we have been able to save very severe shock cases without resorting to blood transfusions or the use of blood serum. Apart from shock cases through loss of blood, we are also doing a good deal of research on the actual effects of shock from blast. We have many such cases now, especially among children, due to the great explosive power of the bombs the Americans are using."

I asked what other research was being done, directly related to the war situation. He took me into a third laboratory where an experiment was being carried out on guinea pigs for testing lime-water as an antidote for phosphorous bombs. "This method is about perfected," Dr. Thach said. "It is simple and efficient, can be applied by anyone and anywhere."

The small body, tied down to the "operating table," quivered slightly as the drops of colorless liquid splashed on its back. Within 40 seconds bluish white smoke started rising from the soaked skin and within a few more seconds there were anguished squeals as the smoke burst into flame, long brilliant sparks leaping between the smoke spirals. A masked, white-gowned figure poured on another liquid which extinguished the flames but did not stop the squeals, then deftly wrapped the whole body in liquid-soaked gauze and it was carried away, still squealing, its place on the "operating table" taken by another small, quivering body. Again some splashes of innocent-looking

liquid, white smoke and squeals as the smoke burst into flames
on the bare body. But this time the squeals trailed away as
liquid from another bottle was poured on, and ended completely as the little body was wrapped in gauze saturated with
the same liquid. Within seconds the bandaged guinea-pig was
nibbling contentedly some greens.

"White phosphorous," explained Dr. Thach, "we have to find
means of countering it that can be available in every village and
can be applied by the peasants themselves. The classic method
is copper sulphate but it's very expensive and can't be made
available on a mass scale. That was used in the first experiment.
In the second, ordinary lime water, available in every Vietnamese village, was used. As you saw, it is more effective. The
pain stops immediately and the burns heal much quicker. It's
a question of getting the mixture absolutely right."

I remarked that I had not heard the Americans were using
phosphorous bombs in the North. "They are using them in the
South," replied Dr. Thach, "and we must reckon on them using
them against our villages as Johnson escalates the war. We
must prepare for the worst."

"We are also studying a simple and practical mask in case
the Americans start using gas or other toxic products." When I
asked for details, he smiled and said: "This is on our secret list.
If the Americans knew what principles we were working on they
would try and counter its efficacy."

Later, on Dr. Thach's advice, I visited the splendidly-
equipped biological research laboratories and saw white mice
being injected by various types of toxic chemicals that the
Americans have been using in South Vietnam, samples of which
have found their way to the North. After a minute dose of one
of the agents, the legs stiffened, the mouse started to stagger and
then fell. "It has the same effect on pigs and buffalo," the re-
searcher explained, "and also on small children and aged, weak
people." The mice that died were passed over to a dissector who
carefully removed minuscule livers, spleens and kidneys and
took blood samples which were passed on back for laboratory
tests. "We can't take any chances," the head of the laboratory
said. "Today it's in the South and tomorrow it may be here."
And obviously any discoveries as to antidotes could be passed

over Radio Hanoi to the South in the form of a scientific commentary!

Returning to my talk with Dr. Thach, he explained that against certain of the chemicals being air-sprayed in the South under the general name of "defoliants," the resulting irritations and inflammations could be cured by extracts of certain medical plants. "We don't always know the reason why but we try to find out. In our situation, it's not for us to try and find complicated, highly specialized methods of treatment, but to find simple and effective treatments within the grasp of our local public health services. People's war imposes on our researchers an effort to find simple remedies, that everyone can use. But the discovery of such remedies requires knowledge of modern, scientific data combined with most detailed laboratory research work and repeated clinical tests, before their popularization."

Certain of these plant extracts, according to Dr. Thach, in clinical tests had proved effective against staphylococci resistant to other antibiotics.

Four-fifths of the patients from the TB hospital and the same proportion of medical personnel had been evacuated to the countryside and this was true of all the other hospitals and medical research centers that I visited. A great deal of expensive laboratory equipment had been removed and mothballed in safe places, until the end of the war. I asked Dr. Thach to what extent the evacuation, mothballing of research equipment and what obviously must have been a large-scale mobilization of medical personnel for the various fronts, would affect normal medical research.

"We will continue research with less sophisticated equipment," Dr. Thach explained, "and we will continue our peacetime public health campaigns. The war will push us to go much faster in this. For two years now, after clinical and successful field tests, we have developed our own subcutaneous injections for cholera, typhoid fever, diphtheria and tetanus. Cholera and smallpox have been wiped out since 1957. The chronic cholera epidemic, which made its appearance in South Vietnam two years ago, did not spread to the North, thanks to our public health campaigns. Typhoid fever and diphtheria have been practically wiped out in those regions where 90 per cent of the population have had subcutaneous injections. An epidemic of infantile paralysis five years ago disappeared, thanks to the Sabin vaccine which our institute of epidemiology continues to produce despite the wartime difficulties. (Later I was to watch the production of this vaccine and control tests on live monkeys.) Serious intestinal diseases caused by insanitary conditions have practically disappeared thanks to the vigor of the public health campaign waged since the American attacks." And, he could have added thanks to his own insistence on the closed double-toilet system, individual wells and other sanitary improvements, referred to elsewhere. "We are also studying the problem of virulent malaria (with which the Americans are having great trouble in the central highlands of South Vietnam) and a solution to this problem, of worldwide importance, will be found. An attempt to use vaccination against helminthiasis is also being tackled."

Then Dr. Thach dealt with a subject very close to his heart —the treatment of tuberculosis with the use of killed BCG vaccine (as opposed to the live vaccine normally used) together with the bacillus subtilis, which he did much to develop and on which he has been invited to present papers at many international conferences on TB.

"Vaccination against TB with killed BCG, studied clinically and experimentally in North Vietnam for almost eight years, because of the ease with which it can be administered and its all-round effectiveness, has greatly contributed to lowering mortality from this disease. In one district of Hanoi, with a population of 100,000, and which has been followed since 1960, the TB mortality rate, as revealed by radio-photography, has fallen from 20.6 per thousand in 1960 to 4.3 per thousand in 1964, that is a reduction of almost 80 per cent in four years. This, despite material conditions which are still difficult.

"The bacillus subtilis," continued Dr. Thach, "which has been known to us since 1952 through the work of Henri and Albot, has been used in big therapeutic doses through numerous injections. Employed alive, either via the lungs, by subcutaneous or even intravenous injections, this bacillus has given surprising results not only for pulmonary and other varieties of TB, but also for leprosy and whooping cough. Administered by nasal inhalations it enables the prevention of epidemics of whooping cough and measles. Our doctors also employed it during the past year with encouraging results in treating tetanus and Japanese encephalitis, as well as in the treatment of infected wounds and burns.

The conversation then turned to the use of various medicinal plants, the effects of which were known but in many cases not the reasons why. Dr. Thach advised me to visit another laboratory where "family planning" experiments were being carried out on white rabbits.

A group of cheerful white-gowned young women met me and escorted me to the rabbit house. Here an experiment was in progress, in which a precisely-measured amount of bluish liquid, fed in through a tube in the rabbit's nose, within a few minutes resulted in an artificial miscarriage, or abortion. They repeated the procedure on several other members of the rabbit colony and showed me charts with dosages and weights and ages of rabbits, the various times it took for satisfactory abortion, according to dosages and so on. The liquid came from a plant, similar to indigo, and was in fact used by the Meo tribespeople to dye their homespun cloth—and to produce abortions. The rabbits showed no ill effects even after prolonged observation, they said, nor did the young Meo tribeswomen. But further investigation would be made before the plant juice would be judged an acceptable "family planning" agent.

In this connection, Dr. Thach explained that it had been known for a long time that certain old women among most of the mountain tribespeople had secret contraceptive concoctions, or at least those which produced abortions. The morals of young people before marriage are, or used to be, notoriously lax but babies born to unwed girls reduced considerably their material value as brides. So the old women who kept the secret of "the pill" were in great demand. But the strictest secrecy was maintained, perhaps at first because of tribal rivalries over such matters, but later because the French Catholic missionaries who established themselves all over the country regarded such practices as outright handiwork of the devil. Punishments were severe if the practitioners were discovered. So the secrets remained in the hands of a few old women and were passed on from family to family. Dr. Thach and his researchers set to work to pry out these secrets, once family planning became an official project.

"It required prolonged political and ideological work," said Dr. Thach, "the tribespeople never yield their secrets easily, especially the older people. It took a long time to gain their confidence, but in the end they began to yield. Now we have some really exciting perspectives." And he went on to describe the effects of one plant which produces temporary sterility after swallowing one single dose and fertility again by a single dose of an antidote, also from a local plant. If the antidote is not taken, sterility remains for all time. The plants have already been found, the juices extracted and they are at present undergoing laboratory tests, whereas the indigo-type abortion-provoker has already passed laboratory and clinical tests. The potentials of the sterility-fertility philter are obviously overwhelming. Dr. Thach is very cautious in professional conversations about the potentials, but is also excited about the prospects of his country capturing a world market in what could be the most popular medicament of our time. "One of the roles of advanced medical science," he said, "is to explain scientifically the almost miraculous properties of many of the medicinal plants. There are certain leaves, for instance, used by the tribespeople that reduce fractures and help the bones set in a fraction of the time of our most advanced methods. Our doctors are studying plants that are very effective against arteriosclerosis, others against malaria and a wide variety of intestinal diseases."

Life expectancy had doubled during the previous decade from 30 to 60 years, the adult death rate having dropped from 20 per thousand in 1955 to six per thousand in 1964, infant mortality in the same period having dropped from 300 to 28 per thousand. "Our people live much longer and die much older and this means we have to do lots of experimental and clinical research in diseases like arteriosclerosis, chronic bronchitis and cancer with which we had little to do in the past," Dr. Thach explained. "We do not let the war interfere with such research. As far as surgery is concerned we gained some world attention

with liver operations and now for the past few years we have
been successfully carrying out throat cancer operations."

Referring again to the importance he and his colleagues in
the Health Ministry attach to the study of medicinal plants and
traditional medicine, Dr. Thach said: "Clinical results obtained
from many of these medicines pose theoretical problems for
which our doctors, chemists and biologists must find the answers
in their laboratories. In this way medical research, medical observation and experimental medicine are closely linked. The
problems are numerous and complicated but if we combine
modern knowledge and practice with the experience of traditional medicine, we hope, bit by bit, to find the answer to problems that baffle us now. To have the most simple and efficient
treatments within the grasp of all, requires a very high level of
modern science."

At the pilot hamlet of Quang An, mentioned in an earlier
chapter, I noticed that 110 medicinal plants growing in the
vicinity had been listed; samples of most of them had been
planted in the small garden of the local clinic. And in the local
pharmacy, alongside one cabinet for modern medicine such as
streptomycin and other antibiotics, there was another cabinet
for traditional medicines, some of them little packets of pow-
dered roots or crumbled leaves. All medicine, western and traditional, was sold only by prescription. The local health officer
assured me that 85 per cent of patients were cured by traditional
medicine. The pharmacy was run by the agricultural cooperative. In the same courtyard as the general clinic was also the
maternity clinic where 48 babies were scheduled for delivery
during 1966.

At Hanoi's University Surgical Hospital, the director, Professor Tung, took me to see a strikingly handsome young lad,
17 years of age, who had recently been brought to Hanoi from
Vinh for a bone graft. He was a third-cycle student, a member
of the school's self-defense unit. Planes came to attack an anti-
aircraft battery near his school. He had rushed out, pointed his
light machine gun at a diving plane and started firing. "Then
there was a tremendous explosion," he said, "and next thing I
was rolling down a small ravine and my leg was covered with
blood." Professor Tung, one of North Vietnam's finest surgeons,

who acted as interpreter, explained that this was a rare case, brought to Hanoi for treatment. "He was a brilliant pupil," he said, "and showed such great courage that it was thought exceptional efforts should be made to save his leg. He lay for two months in a district hospital, but it became evident that only a bone graft of the type we do here could save the leg. We have started work, and will save it. We are using a bit of young calf bone, very suitable for such a case. His leg will be permanently stiff because of the knee injury."

"What do you think about that?" I asked the lad.

"I would willingly give my leg or my life for my country," he said so spontaneously and with such a warm smile that it was clear the words came straight from his heart. The point Professor Tung wanted to make was that it was very rare that surgical cases were brought to Hanoi.

"Almost all operations are carried out in the district hospitals," he said. "It is very rare that patients are brought to provincial hospitals and even rarer to Hanoi. Of the many thousands wounded since the Americans started their bombings, only 31 have come to this hospital, and ours is the chief surgical hospital in Hanoi. The Ministry has made an enormous effort to adapt the district hospitals to our war needs and to train more of our doctors in war surgery. At the present time, we have over 200 district hospitals able to cope with their foreseeable problems."

At the Gia Lam district hospital, which had been moved out of its almost new three-story building in the Hanoi outskirts into a centuries-old Buddhist pagoda, I found that the 100 beds were served by 90 medical personnel, including nine doctors of whom two were surgeons, and ten assistant-doctors (with two years of medical training). The hospital served 33 villages, each of which had a small four-to-five-bed clinic with a qualified nursing sister in charge, and 147 agricultural cooperatives. In the nine months since it had been evacuated to the pagoda, 150 operations had been performed, many of them by the aid of the six-volt bicycle lamp, referred to earlier. Eight of the operations had been for appendicitis and 30 Caesareans.

"In the case of intensified bombardments of the Hanoi area, could you cope?" I asked the doctor in charge.

"There are also two stand-by field hospitals in this district, each with 200 beds," he replied. "With their help, and the local village clinics, we think we can cope." He showed me emergency surgical kits, packed in small leather suitcases, used by mobile teams. The air pump for administering ether was a football bladder, but the surgical kits, made in Germany, looked very efficient. The hospital sterilizer was made from a sand-packed, cut-down petrol drum and could be heated by charcoal or wood. I noticed another modern one, gleaming under its wrappings, standing by for the day when electricity was available. A vacuum pump for extraction of liquids, I noted, was adapted from an ordinary bicycle pump. A cabinet, in which certain medicines had to be maintained at set temperatures, was heated by a petrol lamp. "Improvisation is part of ministerial policy," explained my guide. "We want all our hospital staffs to think in these terms and get used to producing first-class results with the minimum of modern equipment."

On the walls of the pagoda, I noticed a life-size scientific drawing in chalk of certain anatomical aspects in the technique of family planning—free lessons for any patients who cared to glance. The scores of lacquered Buddhas looked on with benign indifference. In any case, the educational wall drawings will lose their importance if Dr. Thach wins out with his sterility-fertility elixir.

Before I completed the check-up on the medical system, I asked Minister Thach what happened with wounded captured pilots.

"The Americans have once again demonstrated their desire for peace by their savage bombardments of Nam Dinh city," he replied, "by the use of their B-52's against Quang Binh province and their escalation of attacks against the suburbs of Hanoi and Haiphong. The list of our children, men and women, the sick, lepers, TB patients, that they have killed is a long one. Also the list of schools, hospitals, homes and roads that they've destroyed. They are criminals and deserve to be punished as such. Nevertheless, if they are captured wounded, we treat them with exactly the same care that we give to our own patients."

Chapter 7

WOMEN AT WAR

When North Vietnam's leaders start to speak of the role their women are playing their faces take on an ecstatic look, their eyes go moist, their voices husky. If that is an exaggeration, it is a small one. Not only the leaders, but most of the men act the same way when the subject is raised. With this war, Vietnamese women have come really into their own. In a few, short years, they have sprung out of the underprivileged status imposed by centuries of feudalism, capped by colonialism, into their leading role in national life today. Before they were indispensable only as wives and mothers. Now they are indispensable as economic producers, as a great labor force, as farm and factory managers, directors of hospitals and, where need be, as combatants. Above all, they represent the great economic force that has freed the men for what is universally referred to as the "front"—whether it is the actual combat front, the hard, dangerous construction jobs in the mountains, or the road-building and repair fronts.

The women are glorying and thriving in their new role. They have been swirled up in the whirlwind of the new revolution that is sweeping the countryside and shaking it to its roots. Probably Vietnamese women will never be the same again. They are now the "more than equals" in Vietnamese society, the real indispensables. They have earned themselves a new status and are living up to their new role with dignity, responsibility, courage—and gaiety. Above all, they remain very feminine despite having assumed very masculine responsibilities.

"When the pirates come the women must also take to arms," is an ancient Vietnamese saying. It was quoted to me many times in explaining the heroic role of Vietnamese women throughout history, starting with the two sisters, Trung Trac and Trung Nhi, who in 40 A.D. put themselves at the head of an army which rallied the people and drove the Han (Chinese)

invaders out of the country. The Trung sisters founded a king-
dom which lasted three years. Then the Hans came back.

Over the past few years, women in the North have become
relatively emancipated. Feudal customs still die hard in some
of the villages. Parents still want to arrange marriages; many
still want their daughters to lacquer their teeth and wear button-
at-the-neck blouses and stick to such traditional women's work
as planting out rice seedlings, looking after ducks, selling farm
products in the market and so on. But in general, the young
people have broken away from that. According to the latest
available data, women occupy 48 per cent of jobs in light industry, 45 per cent in handicrafts, 38 per cent in administration,
32 per cent in state trading organs, and 23 per cent in heavy
industry.

And that was the situation before the American bombers
struck. By now the women are doing the overwhelmingly greater
part of productive work—70 to 80 per cent of the work in agriculture alone. Not only unskilled work. Education Minister
Nguyen Van Huyen had talked about the specialized training
courses in agriculture, opened at village level for women, after
the American attacks started and the men took off for the fronts.

"The participation of women in collective labor has been the
basis for our development," said Le Thu, the be-spectacled,
gentle-faced woman from the international affairs department
of the Women's Association in Hanoi. "In many cases, after 12
years of taking part in collective labor, they have reached the
level of higher education. As far as salaries are concerned we
have complete equality with the men, equal pay for equal work.
We receive State aid for the family during pregnancy, paid
leave before and after child-birth, etc. That's something completely new in the history of our country. One great source of
joy for us women is that our children, all our children, girls and
boys, go to school. In the old days the girls had to look after
their little brothers and sisters. In any case, there was usually
no room for them in the schools. All this has greatly contributed
to the real emancipation of our women and explains the enthusiasm with which we have thrown ourselves into the new tasks
imposed by the war. On March 19, 1965, after the first American
attacks, the leaders of our country allotted three principal tasks

to the women: Stimulate production and defend the motherland, insure the day-to-day life of the people, take part in
combat.

"The main task is to work in production. In our society now
there is a new distribution of work. Women are very apt for
productive work, especially in agriculture and light industry.
When the men take off, guns in hand, for the front, it's the
women who must replace them in the factories and fields. When
the rear is solid, the men at the front are more assured, they
feel fortified for the struggle. If the enemy comes where we are
working, we women will also engage in combat. That is clear.

"For us women, by taking part in production our fundamental rights are asserted, equality with the men in all spheres,
in technical and administrative capacity, and in education."

She explained with a sigh that some of her sisters were not
satisfied with the "passive" role of being mainly producers. They
felt that point three of the leaders' directive was the main thing;
they wanted to get into the fight with guns in their hands, or
at least pass the ammunition, care for the wounded, look after
transport and supplies. But Directive 99, which the Lao Dong
(Workers Party) central committee had approved in relation
to women's activities, had stressed that production was the main
task and also that women should "do everything to insure the
well-being of the old people, the women and children, because
the war increases their hardships every day." Based on the tasks
set, the Women's Association had launched a movement called
the "three responsibilities," parallel to the "three readies"
adapted by the youth. Textually this included:

(1) Replace the men, free them for combat duties.

(2) Take charge of the family, encourage husband and children to leave for the front.

(3) Serve or take part in combat when necessary.

These three points calmed the feelings of even the most
ardent of the members, according to Le Thu, because it was
also made clear that the Americans having launched the challenge by attacking North and South of the 17th parallel, the
question of reunification of the country was on the order of the
day. The main content of the national task was defined as "defend production and continue to build socialism, defend the

North and liberate the South for the reunification of the country." As far as the women were concerned, there was to be no more nonsense about paying lip-service to the idea that the war was to be fought in two isolated compartments. For them there was one single front, one single national task. Arms would not be laid down, husbands and sons would not be called home until the Americans had called off their attacks against the North, been chased out of the South and the country had been reunified.

This was made even more clear when Le Thu said: "The most characteristic trait is that the revolutionary and patriotic spirit of the women is on the upsurge. The will to take part in the liberation of the South is a very strong motive for our women. Two months after the movement was launched, over two million women had adhered to it, in the plains as in the mountains, from the 17th parallel to the most distant coastal islands."

She went on to explain that in order to "steel themselves and learn to acquire revolutionary virtues," women from the non-attacked areas went to Quang Binh and Vinh Linh provinces where the fight was hottest, to learn how their sisters tilled the fields and brought in the harvest despite the daily bombardments. "The leading comrades from down there come here to make reports. We send cadres from our Association down there and we publish booklets to publicize the experiences of the women in the front line. Wherever the Americans attack they find women as heroic in combat as in production."

In my own travels, I came across young women everywhere who had distinguished themselves in combat, often in most unusual circumstances—the young woman at the Ghep ferry, who seized the tiller under enemy fire after the helmsman had been killed and his replacement badly wounded; the fragile girl who carried boxes of ammunition twice her own weight during a vital battle for the Ham Rong bridge; another from the same unit who rushed to the river bank under exploding bombs to save a barge filled with rice. Teen-age girls made repeated trips under exploding bombs and machine-gun fire to carry kindergarten toddlers to safety. Scores and scores of girls blushed, embarrassed to the tips of their hair, when their colleagues related their exploits to me. Many villages in the coastal areas now have tiny war museums, with bits of American planes and pilot's equipment and the photos of those who have sacrificed their lives in combat. A high proportion of the latter are village girls.

I saw young women from a Nam Dinh fruit-canning plant doing most realistic bayonet drills; one line with bayonetted rifles in hand lunging ferociously at another line of girls who had nothing in their hands, but expertly parried the thrusts and tried to wrench the weapons away from their "opponents." They are slim, beautiful girls, but strong as spring steel. In any sneak landing attempts, the Americans would find themselves confronted by tens of thousands of such young women, well versed in hand-to-hand combat. At the fruit-canning plant, 80 per cent of the workers were young women who also made up 90 per cent of the self-defense corps, most of the men workers being on the elderly side. They had permanent anti-aircraft positions set up along the river bank, including 12.7 and 20mm heavy machine guns all manned by girls, already veterans of 16 battles to keep planes away from their factory. The same thing is true in Haiphong where the factory self-defense units in many cases were almost exclusively composed of women, well trained in the arms they were expected to use. The fact that the deputy chief of the Liberation Army in the South is a woman, Nguyen Thi Dinh, was a source of satisfaction and inspiration for the women of the North, I found.

"Our women," continued Le Thu, "now represent 70 to 80 per cent of the labor force in the agricultural cooperatives. There, where the fight is very tough, the women are very proud; they have promised never to retreat. Production today demands not only sweat but blood. In the most dangerous spots there are groups of young girls, the vanguard, the most courageous, to continue the work. Their slogan is: 'Never Retreat.'

"Very often, leaving for the front, the husbands prepare shelters for their wives, alongside the field where they will be working. But the latter rarely use them, only when the bombers are right over their heads. Sometimes the planes hang around for a long time in the same spot. But they stay there too, to snatch away the harvest. There are cases where the bombs fall while the women are carrying back the sheaves, the blast sending them in one direction, the sheaves in another. But as soon as they are on their feet again, they gather up the sheaves and carry on. In such moments, they tell us, they feel especially strongly united with their husbands at the front. Wherever they work, there are self-defense units on permanent duty and first-aid teams to help the wounded. When we speak of the 'battle for the harvest', it is no longer against nature that we must fight but against a very cruel, very dangerous enemy."

Even the fact that the women have had to take over agricultural production has contributed to the "technical revolution" in the countryside. It has speeded up the drive to lighten physical work. Instead of bashing the grain out of the sheaves by hand as formerly, there are now treadle-operated threshing machines. Instead of the back-breaking work of hand-weeding, there are small wheeled implements that are pushed along between the rows. Instead of husking the rice by pounding it in a pestle, there are now mechanical huskers in most cooperatives. Most "revolutionary" of all, as far as the women are concerned, is that instead of carrying the sheaves back in baskets suspended from each end of a bamboo carrying pole, as has been done for centuries, the sheaves are now hauled in small handcarts, the terraces between the rice fields having been specially enlarged to permit their passage. Widening of the terraces has gone hand in hand with a changed irrigation system and the work of leveling off the fields, so that dozens of patch fields formerly separated by narrow terraces because of the different levels are now transformed into one perfectly level field. The crazy patch-work mosaic of fields and terraces, so typical of the past, is disappearing in favor of large, rectangular or square fields, alternately intersected by irrigation channels and the new wide, and often metal-surfaced bund paths—a very important aspect of the "revolution."

"Our women are very glad to learn the new methods," continued Le Thu. "Their husbands will have plenty to learn from them when they return. They take part in courses for technical improvement. They plant the rows of rice seedlings closer, in straight lines to enable mechanical weeding, in east-west rows to enable the sun to do its work better; seed selection is better to increase yields. It is very largely because our women have mastered these new techniques that many cooperatives reached five tons per hectare in 1965; also because our women are very hard-working. In certain provinces, some women got in up to 400 work-days for the year."

A work-day is based on a quota of ten points which represents a certain area ploughed, planted, weeded or other defined tasks. In certain cooperatives that I visited, there were women who often earned 30 to 35 points a day. Before the American attacks, when there was a manpower surplus on the land, it was rare for a co-op member to get in more than 170 work-days a year and the average was far below that, especially in the coastal plains and the Red River delta.

For their part in the two-year economic plan, the "three-responsibilities" women in the countryside had pledged themselves to push for more mechanization, to reduce physical effort but intensify the work done, to attain five tons of rice per hectare all over the country, to learn to plough properly and prepare the seed in the seedling nurseries, to learn how to thatch the roofs with rice straw after the harvest, and also to learn the elements of carpentry. Their menfolk were really in for surprises!

As for industry, the gentle Le Thu continued: "There the task is quickly to train new semi-skilled workers. Those who are already skilled take on novices to work alongside them for training. There are also evening courses in different specialties. To train teams of women capable of management jobs, there are weeks and even months when they practice self-management. That is to say, during one week or one month, the women themselves take over management. The training of technical and management cadres has been very successful. The trade unions helped a great deal." She went on to cite the example of Hanoi's "March 8" textile mill, where 1,906 of the "three-responsibilities" workers had mastered two or three specialties. The principle of the drive for technical improvement was that not only must they improve their qualifications in their own specialty but they should learn one or two more, so they would be interchangeable.

"Two hundred weavers," continued Le Thu, "have not only become skilled weavers but they have learned to work at the spinning machines as well. Others have learned to repair the machines, exclusively a man's job before. They completed 1965 with two million meters of textiles above the plan."

Finally, Mrs. Le Thu explained that following the advice of President Ho the women in the North have engaged in a competition with their sisters in the South to accomplish the following tasks, known as the "five pledges":

(1) To fight well against the Americans and their puppets.

(2) To produce well and to exercise strict economy in production.

(3) To feed the war wounded well and look after them.

(4) To carry out family tasks well, to look after and educate the children properly.

(5) To be virtuous and behave properly.

"These are the pledges undertaken by the women of North and South, by the women of Hanoi and Saigon, by the women from our mountainous areas and those of the high plateaux. On March 8, 1967 (International Women's Day) reports will be presented on the results." And Le Thu repeated that a desperate struggle has started for the reunification of the country. "We will do everything possible that the country be reunited, that the days of misery in the South will soon be over, that the Americans will be chased out of Vietnam. This will to struggle is universal among our women." She recalled again the role played by the Trung sisters in the first century and by another Vietnamese woman warrior, Trieu Trinh Nuong, who during the Wu dynasty in 248 A.D. put herself at the head of an army, together with her brother, and inflicted a heavy defeat on the Chinese occupiers. And about the heroism of Vietnamese women many times since.

"During the first resistance war," she said, "our women suffered greatly. The memories of suffering and bereavement are still not effaced from our hearts. Every village has its memories of atrocities. That is why, this time, our women together with the men are ready to fight for five, ten, 15 or more years if necessary. There is also the question of our feelings toward our sisters in the South. We will do everything to shorten their sufferings and we will try to follow their heroic example. We are all of us ready to sacrifice ourselves for them."

President Ho Chi Minh

Defenders of the Ham Rong bridge: women's self-defense unit (below), gun crew (right).

Self-defense unit at "March 8" textile factory, Hanoi.

"All clear" for this truck convoy after air raid.

US jet planes approach.

The alert is sounded on a village tom-tom.

*Yen Phuc village near the Ham Rong bridge,
victim of US air raids.*

Ruins of TB hospital Number 71 at Thanh Hoa.

Remains of kindergarten attached to textile workers' apartments, Nam Dinh.

These workers' homes in Nam Dinh were completed in mid-1964, destroyed in mid-1965.

Bikes can carry half a ton of supplies 20 miles a day for weeks on end. As with horses, they require no fuel.

A US jet plane goes to the airplane cemetery.

Vietnamese children.

A tryst at Hanoi's thousand-years-old Mot Cot (Single Pillar) Pagoda.

The "March 8" textile factory before evacuation (above) and after (right).

Looms now weave in makeshift huts.

The older women now do the plowing.

And the older men now make fishing nets.

Going to school.

Comunication trenches in the classroom lead to shelters in the fields.

A hospital research laboratory evacuated to nearby pagoda.

Alert interrupts church service in this Catholic fishing village.

"Hanoi Hannah"
broadcasts to GI's in
South Vienam.

Hanoi billboards ridicule President's Johnson's "peace offers."

Defense units include Polytechnic University students . . .

. . . and Hanoi factory workers.

One of Hanoi's open air restaurants before air attacks began.

A rare sight in Hanoi today, lovers at Thong Nhat lake.

General Vo Nguyen Giap,
Defense Minister and
Commander-in-Chief of the
Vietnam Peoples' Army.

The author and his wife with
Prime Minister Pham Van Dong
and Ho Chi Minh.

These last words of Le Thu might have sounded banal. But they were not—not from the mouth of this gentle-faced, quiet-spoken woman. One knows that only too often Vietnamese women of her type, tender-mouthed, soft-voiced, delicate and exquisitely feminine, have faced death and worse with the same sweet, shy smile on their lips.

The Vietnamese women have accepted an enormous burden on their slim shoulders. Like the girl ammunition carrier at Ham Rong bridge, they all seem to be carrying twice their own weight. They have to replace the man at work in field and factory but still be good mothers at home—and in many cases good children as well, for there are often the old people as well as the children to look after. To a certain extent their burdens are eased by crèches and nursery schools, but the war comes even there also. Normally the older women could look after the crèches but when the planes come, strong, young people are needed to carry a whole armful of children at once, and move quickly. If there are not such strong, competent people in charge, mothers will come rushing back from the fields every time a plane is heard. All this means careful, rational organization. I have seen crèches in some villages where at the approach of planes babies are lowered on a cord and pulley device four at a time, each in separate padded baskets, into deep shelters located just under their normal resting place.

There is, incidentally, to be a wholesale reduction in babies, even apart from the family-planning campaigns among the already married and even before Dr. Thach's sterility-fertility philter is perfected. Apart from the indefinite absence of a large proportion of young men of marriageable age, young people have been officially advised to reflect carefully before falling in love, to reflect even more deeply before marrying and to think and think again before having children—for the duration of the war. It is recommended that young women should not marry before 23 and men not before 25. In case human disciplines waver, social censure insures that, by and large, such advice is followed. At present, 8,000,000 of North Vietnam's 17,000,000 population are under 15 years of age, but the proportion of infants will be radically diminished in the years that come.

At the "March 8" textile mill, in the outskirts of Hanoi, officially inaugurated on March 8, 1965, just a month after the systematic air attacks started against the DRV, I found that women accounted for 77 per cent of a total labor force of 6,500. It is the biggest textile mill after that at Nam Dinh. Enrollment in the "three readies" was 100 per cent and 2,000 workers were members of a self-defense battalion, a section of which permanently manned the defense positions. There were many gaps in sections where machines had been evacuated to become the nucleus of small plants scattered around the countryside. Workers' flats had been built in the neighborhood to house 3,400 of the workers but these had now been abandoned except for self-defense units designated for their defense, and their families. (In general, casualties from air raids are kept low because people in exposed areas are encouraged to live in single-story dwellings from which they can be in air raid shelters within seconds—a real necessity when planes come at supersonic speeds and the first warnings are from anti-aircraft shells and exploding bombs. Also there is no danger of being buried under ruins.)

The system of shelters seemed excellent, with brick-lined zigzag trenches leading from the exits of all the factory buildings, along which workers could rush, with their heads below surface level, to reinforced shelters in the fields, well away from the factory buildings. In addition, the whole area inside the factory compound was dotted with the cylindrical, individual shelters which are now standard throughout North Vietnam. These are mass-produced, concrete cylinders with a floor at the bottom and open at the top, which are sunk into the ground and comfortably accommodate a single person. They are perfectly shaped to resist blast and, unless they receive a direct hit, the inmate is reasonably safe. The closed bottom keeps out water almost always present in the subsoil of the plains area. The quantity of air inside would give a reasonable time for rescuers to dig their way through any earth which might be thrown over the top by a near miss. All major and secondary roads are lined with such shelters for travelers to jump into at any moment. The same is true in the main streets of the villages. They are a very effective supplement to the reinforced, family or communal shelters which have been built everywhere people work or live.

"Every meter of cloth is a bullet against the enemy, is our

slogan," a young woman in the weaving section said. Rifles on racks stood at the head of every line of machines and canvas kits with red crosses on them were also in evidence. The mill was working on a 24-hour, seven-day week basis, with the obvious aim of squeezing out every meter of cloth before "the worst happens." A system of red and blue lights for air raid warnings was installed throughout, more effective than sirens in view of the tremendous clatter the weaving machines make.

"All the young men without exception wanted to go to the front," my guide from the factory management said. "Some of the experienced technicians and a few other key, skilled workers, had to be kept back. But we had to organize courses to explain that production was also a front-line task. Otherwise we would not have had a man left. Thousands of our girls have now learned to do jobs they never touched before, repairing machines, power lines and so on."

The day after the first bombs fell on the outskirts of the capital, I called at Radio Hanoi to have a talk with "Hanoi Hanna," as the American G.I.'s in South Vietnam call the girl who beams a special English-language broadcast to try and persuade them they are fighting for a wrong and hopeless cause. In fact "Hanna" are two pretty young women. Thu Huong (Autumn Fragrance) was on duty, when I called. Her colleague, Cambridge-educated "Perfumed Orchid," was off duty that day. As with most other Hanoi mothers, Thu Huong's children were evacuated to the countryside. I asked what she thought about the threat to Hanoi. Her reply, in English, could have been the national reaction: "Even if they destroy Hanoi, we are fully prepared to carry on the struggle until final victory. The Americans can never win because our people are absolutely united and well prepared morally and materially to continue the struggle in all circumstances."

Chapter 8

OF BEES AND BULKHEADS

"We have taken vows to love the bees as we would our husbands," blushingly confided the charming, round-faced bee-keeper, as she gently extracted a honeycomb frame from one of a dozen or so gaily painted hives, laid out under flowering longan trees. Golden honey started oozing out and bees, almost wagging their tails, crawled over the well-kept hands of their mistress-lover. The term, Queen Bee, began to take on a different meaning!

"You have to treat them tenderly, lovingly, lovingly," she said, as she took out two more frames, handing each in turn to her colleague who, after gently brushing off the bees, scraped the crust from the honey cells and placed three frames in a metal container. A handle was turned, the frames whirled and the honey splashed out to funnel down and neatly fill a one-liter jar. Duong Thi Ve, a very pretty girl of 19 in a blue jacket, who had explained about the vows, and her colleague, Bui Thi Thua, a year her junior, both graduates from a local Technical School, were now in charge of bee-farming at Le Chau village, Hung Yen province, about 60 miles south of Hanoi.

"How is it the bees don't sting?" I asked, used to bee-keepers armed with masks and gloves for such operations, or working under a screen of smoke.

"Because we don't harm them," replied Duong Thi Ve. "We educate them very carefully. We handle them gently, never move them brusquely, never open the hives when it is too hot or too cold, we put the frames in the hives very carefully so that no bees are crushed, and we place the hives in advantageous positions in the garden where the most fragrant perfumes reach the bees. In general, we try to create the best conditions for them to go about their work."

After much prodding from her colleague, Duong Thi Ve began to sing in a thin, sweet voice a little ditty about "relations between man and bees" which set out in rhyme and tune the principles of how to make bees love humans.

Their "Vietcong" sisters in the South had succeeded in doing just the opposite—training a very fierce type of outsize, non-honey-producing bee to hate humans, at least to attack any strangers approaching their villages. Whole districts were protected by a formidable "air force," an average of 200 nests of warrior-bees per hamlet.*

The two girls explained some of the mysteries of their profession—how, now by helping, now by swindling the bees, they had increased by many times the production of honey. They demonstrated a small machine, shaped like a waffle-iron, on which they turned out daily 5,000 sheets of "prefabricated honeycomb," made from beeswax and paraffin.

"These save the bees 40 days of work," the blushing, smiling, enthusiastic Miss Ve said. "It gives them all that more time out among the flowers. They are much more contented than bees that have to make their own cells." She pointed out that the machine-made cells were of a standard hexagonal shape and size. "If they were bigger the drones would get in and eat up all the honey." The bees, it appeared, did not object and went on industriously filling in the man-made cells with honey as if they were all their own work, but at least covering up each cell with their own wax. "It means that the bees can go out to work every day of our five seasons. Before, people here got honey from only one flower season, about 20 to 25 kilograms a hive of six frames. Now we get five times that, an average of 100 to 125 kilograms per hive a year."

I was offered a small glass of "bees' milk" which I was assured had an invigorating effect and was highly recommended for elderly people. It looked and tasted like honey and cream and I downed it at a gulp. On closer inspection, I found I had drunk the larvae of a score or so of bees, steeped in honey. I expressed the hope that it was only the useless drones that I had downed, but the girls assured me that it did not matter. They had found ways of forcing the queen bees to vastly increase their output of

* See Wilfred G. Burchett, *Vietnam: Inside Story of the Guerilla War,* N.Y., International Publishers, 1965, pp. 202–205.

larvae. A regular portion of "bees' milk" was set aside for President Ho and other elderly veterans.

Not only had the evil, old smells been abolished from Le Chau village, but they had been replaced by the fragrance of flowers and honey which reached the nostrils from afar. This was now true of scores of other villages in the region. Bee-keeping was something new, but rapidly expanding. The first dozen hives at Le Chau had produced 1.2 tons of honey in 1965, providing enough funds to set up another hundred in 1966. The local cooperative manager explained that for every dong* earned from the honey, another ten dong were earned by the increased yields of fruit and vegetables since the busy bees had been at work insuring that no flowers were left unfertilized.

That part of Hung Yen province was famed for its longan trees; they lined the river and canal banks and the roadsides, surrounded the houses in every village. The fruit, about the size of a plum with a rough skin and big black pip, with sweet and juicy, transparent flesh, is much appreciated in Southeast Asia. And of all the great variety of flowers in the area, the bees prefer that of the longan: "The income from longans for our hamlet before bees was 20,000 dong," the co-op manager said. "Now it is 100,000. It's the same with squashes, cucumbers and lots of other products."

The landscape around Le Chau is particularly beautiful and fertile these days. Villages and individual houses are surrounded by greenery. Apart from the ever-present, graceful bamboo, there are the longans and litchis (the latter with a similar and much appreciated fruit), orange and grapefruit trees, bananas and papayas. Every hamlet has lotus-bedecked ponds and when the fish come up for air and insects, they are so numerous that one sees only swaying fish heads and lotus leaves. Frames built out over the ponds support vines of cucumber, squash and other gourd-like vegetables that flourish in the area, all covered with large yellow flowers at the time of my visit. One had the impression of harmoniously integrated cycles of nature, everything neat and orderly, with the bees very much in evidence and the fragrance of flowers and honey everywhere in the air.

* One dong is equivalent to about 28½ cents, US.

Hung Yen was formerly one of the major "problem provinces" of North Vietnam. It forms a rectangle with its whole western boundary marked by the Red River, the major river of the North. The southern boundary runs almost parallel to the Bamboo Canal which connects the lower reaches of the Red River with Haiphong, to the northeast. It is an almost perfectly flat area "without mountains, forest or sea," as the provincial Lao Dong secretary pointed out, most other provinces having at least one of those three natural features. The greatest drawback is that it is like a draining board, tilted downward from north to south. Statistically, its misfortune is that in the north, roughly along the Hanoi-Haiphong highway, the land is 7.5 meters above sea level, whereas in the south, it is only 1.2 meters above sea level. The difference in levels has caused endless cycles of drought in the north and floods in the south ever since recorded history. In flood years, which were often, the water poured down from the north, sweeping over and destroying the retaining walls of irrigation dikes, to bank up in the south, placing the fields there under anything upwards of a meter of water. Both the Red River and the Bamboo Canal run bankers at such times; they refuse to accept any more water. Regions in the south lay waterlogged for months on end.

"In the south the crops rot in the field, in the north they're burned black by the sun," is one of the popular sayings in Hung Yen. Fields of growing rice were referred to as "dream crops" because you could only "dream" of harvesting them, since flood or drought had wiped them out so often. But the battle against nature formed tough militant spirits among the peasants, who played a vigorous role in the first resistance war.

"In the great famine of 1945, when two million people died in the North, we only lost 10,000 in Hung Yen," explained Quynh, the local Lao Dong party secretary.

"Why?"

"Because the people attacked the Japanese grain stores and helped themselves."

Quynh should have known, because I heard from other sources that he was one who organized the attacks. It was Quynh, a small, smiling man of inexhaustible energy, who had taken me to meet the bees and their keepers, because he was proud of this new money-maker in his province. Nearly three years previously, he had taken me to see the first pumping stations in the province and the first fish-raising projects, the latter so successful that Chinese fish-breeding experts, who had come to help, looked and praised and went away again with new ideas for their own ponds. In the first resistance, Hung Yen province was decorated by President Ho as a "model guerrilla province," despite the lack of mountains, jungle or sea. "You are rich in people," "Uncle Ho" had said and this had been the guiding line for Quynh and 17,000 other Communists, only 5,000 of whom survived the war.

"At the end of the war when we were asked for an inventory of equipment in our province," Quynh said, "all we could muster was one old syringe for injection of pigs and another primitive machine for making ice cream. No other instruments or machines. As for educational standards, we were not only almost completely illiterate, but because of the terrible conditions of the struggle, living in holes in the ground, cadres isolated from each other, many of us had forgotten many ordinary words in our spoken language."

Driving through the province today, as I did, from north to south and south to north and east-west at several levels, it looked as if it were about due for another "model province" decoration. It is a study in geometry today, squares and rectangles, intersected by straight lines of varying width, according to whether one is looking at major roads and canals, or secondary roads and bund paths between the fields, and subsidiary irrigation channels. The province has been "tilted" back, if not to abolish the difference in levels between north and south, at least to render the difference harmless. This has been done by setting up a network of pumping stations and an average of three electric pumps for every one of the province's 155 villages. The water moves from north to south in an orderly, controlled manner and if it moves too fast it is sent back from south to north again by the pumps. The flat lands are divided by "bulkheads" that trap and restrain unruly waters, the "bulkheads" being in the form of the bund roads and tracks built up well above the level of the fields they divide.

Why "bulkheads"? "Here, as in all other provinces bordering

the Red River, we must prepare for the worst," replied Quynh, and his face was unusually somber.

There was no need to ask what the "worst" meant in this case. It had been known in Hanoi for some time previously that the Americans had dug out old French plans, never put into effect, for breaching the Red River dikes and causing floods of catastrophic proportions. In July and August 1965 there had been systematic and intensive bombing attacks against dams and irrigation systems which tapered off only after criticism in many countries allied to the USA. "You know," said Quynh, reading my thoughts, "that warships are now built on a sort of cell principle so that the flooding of one section from bomb or torpedo damage below the waterline can be limited to the affected area. The same system can be applied to flood damage. In any case, it fits in with our technical revolution in the countryside. Leveling off the fields makes possible maximum and most economic use of irrigation. Our province is now completely irrigated. The bund roads are part of the new inter-provincial system. The graveled paths between the fields are for the new handcarts."

The Volga car in which we were traveling flashed along a south-north asphalted road. At regular intervals a two-lane gravel road crossed ours at right angles, and parallel to it a main canal, five or ten yards wide. In between these roads and canals were a dozen or more alternating yard-wide irrigation channels and "bulkhead" paths for the handcarts, the earth removed in digging the canals and channels obviously having served for roads and paths. Later, when we turned south again and drove along the left bank of the Red River, it was comforting to see that a second system of huge dikes had been built, still higher than the banks of the Red River and parallel to it. The intervening space would serve to trap river waters in case "the worst happened."

The work done, even since my previous visit, one could only describe as fantastic, especially as it was all done with picks and spades and wicker baskets. I asked what were the results in terms of production figures.

"Our two main agricultural crops are rice and jute," Quynh replied, and he gave me the figures for 1959, a reasonably good year, and 1965: In the latter year, rice production was 76,000 tons, as compared with 19,000 tons in 1959; and 11,000 tons of jute as against only 75 tons in 1959.

"In 1959, we were not even self-supporting in rice," Quynh said. "We had to be helped by the state. In 1965, we sold 46,000 tons of rice to the state, plus 3,500 tons of pigs and 250 tons of fish."

In almost every village we passed through or sighted from the road, Quynh had personal reminiscences of the "first resistance." From this one, a notable ambush had been laid; in that one he had been trapped by the enemy and, disguised as an old woman, had been hidden by the peasants; here a band of redoubtable women guerrillas had their headquarters; there he had lived in a culvert for a week, children bringing him food and in that one —and he turned to his wife, sitting beside him in the Volga— he had met and married a revolutionary from Thanh Hoa province. Their daughter, "Miss Moonlight," also in the car with us, was conceived in another of the many villages we passed. With us also was Quang Huy, another notable son of Hung Yen who, for years past, has directed North Vietnam's Documentary Film Studios. Normally a man of few words, Quang Huy, on one occasion as we were traveling along the Hanoi-Haiphong road near the province's northern border, was inspired by the flood of reminiscences to recall how one of his several "deaths" took place in that area.

As a cameraman, he had been given the task of filming the blowing up of a train on the Haiphong-Hanoi line. It was an "impossible" assignment. There was a military post every kilometer along the parallel road and railway line, and patrols between the posts all the time. Before any train passed, an old locomotive with an "expendable" Vietnamese crew was sent ahead of freight trains to detonate any mines. Quang Huy accepted the task on condition that the prize was really worthwhile. It must really be spectacular and film-worthy—he would only consider a train of gasolene cisterns. This was agreed. For over a week, he and local villagers went about their preparations. Word came from Haiphong of the date, approximate hour, and weight, of a cistern train. The weight was important because the train-sabotage experts set a delicate fuse based on the extent to which the rails would be depressed by the weight of the train. In this way the lighter, "expendable" locomotive would not detonate it.

Quang Huy himself chose the site where the explosion would take place, one with a clear field of view for his camera to film the whole sequence. The day before, he arranged to have himself "buried" in a cemetery close to the railway. A long procession of "mourners" turned out with trumpeters ahead and wailers behind. He was lowered in the coffin, the earth filled in and stamped down, but with a fine rubber tube leading from the coffin to the surface. In the miraculous way which only the Vietminh (and now the "Vietcong") have, the saboteurs evaded the patrols to plant their pressure mine. But inside the coffin things had gone wrong. Somehow the tube had got twisted or fouled. In any case, the tube end in the coffin had become too short. Quang Huy suffocated and lost consciousness, he "died" until with a last convulsive effort he must have jerked the tube free and intuitively got the end into his mouth and started to breathe again. When he recovered consciousness he freed himself from the coffin and gradually removed the earth until he had a hole behind the tombstone from which he could use his camera.

I have since seen the dramatic results of this escapade in Quang Huy's fabulous documentary film of resistance in the Red River delta area. The cistern train rolls smoothly along until the explosion blows the locomotive off the tracks; and then the spectacular almost leisurely telescoping of the cistern cars, each in turn exploding into fire, great billows of black smoke and flame gradually enveloping the lot. The timing for everything was perfect and Quang Huy, with his camera, escaped into the local village tunnel system (which the peasants had worked on throughout the night to approach the graveyard) while French patrols scoured the area.

"This has always been a bad province for invaders," Quynh remarked. "In the 13th century the head of the Mongol invaders, Toa Do, left his bones here. After the fighting started at the end of 1946, the French set up 480 posts in over 700 hamlets, but by the time of Dien Bien Phu we had wiped out every single one. Two hundred of our hamlets had also been completely razed—everything, from chickens to buffalo and cooking pots to ploughs, completely destroyed."

This time Hung Yen was one of the few provinces that had not been bombed, there being neither bridges nor industry to attract the bombers. But all school and hospital buildings had been evacuated as a precaution, something which obviously caused pangs of pain to the party secretary.

"When we took over," Quynh said, "there was not a single doctor in the province, the head of the public health service had the rank of trained nurse. There were a few first-cycle schools, and one second-cycle school in neighboring Thai Binh province, but it had to serve three provinces. Now we have a first-cycle school in every cooperative, a second-cycle school in every one of our 155 villages and ten third-cycle schools, plus a Teachers Training College for second-cycle teachers. We have experimental agricultural stations in every village, 24 engineers, 446 specialists who have graduated from the secondary specialist colleges and 1,400 skilled, agricultural workers. Every cooperative has an average of 80 low-level technical workers who can handle irrigation, the use of fertilizers, seed selection, and can supervise sections of road- and canal-building operations, and so forth. Our technical revolution is in full swing.

"As for public health, we have 30 doctors and 184 assistant doctors, one of the latter attached to every village and the rest serving in the district centers and provincial capital." Among other figures he quoted was 1,200 midwives with Health Ministry qualifications, an average of nearly eight per village. It was in Hung Yen during a previous visit, I recalled, that I had found a village averaging 11 children per family and that Quynh had told me of a woman who had given birth 25 times and "had lost three years due to the resistance." I asked about family planning. He smiled:

"You have seen the churches in nearly every village. This was the first province to have been Catholicized. Our peasant women tend to regard children as gifts from heaven. In the old days infant mortality was so high, often 50 per cent, that mothers felt they should have as many babies as possible in order that five or six might grow up. For some time past we have been educating the people, starting with our own cadres, first as to the economic desirability of family planning, then as to the technique. Our midwives these days are busier teaching mothers how not to have babies than delivering them. We consider that four children ought to be the limit and we encourage families with more than that to emigrate to the virgin lands of the northwest. If the war spreads it is safer there; it is also healthier, and there's more room."

Quynh was justifiably proud of the pumping stations and every now and again we stopped while he explained the particular functions of one or another of them. They were almost all double-purpose stations, ready to drain off surplus water and divert it into the irrigation channels or to build up the level in the latter and direct the flow to the water-short areas.

We visited the Teachers Training College. Until recently it had been housed in a fine two-story building in the outskirts of the provincial capital. Now the building had been abandoned, the college students distributed among five other buildings—a Buddhist pagoda, a Buddhist temple (the difference being that pagodas house Buddhas, temples are erected to honor some meritorious historic personalities), a Catholic church, a building given up by a cooperative and another the students had built themselves. We visited students in the latter and in the pagoda. Altogether there were 840 of whom 700-odd were girls with serious, delicate faces. Ages of the budding teachers ranged from 17 to 35 but the majority were very young. All had completed seven years of general education either at school or in complementary courses and were doing an intensive three-year course to graduate as secondary teachers.

Some wrinkled, brown-clad bonzes gathered around the pagoda and assured us that the Lord Buddha would be content at the meritorious use to which the pagoda was being put; traditionally the pagodas were centers of learning.

A girl student stood up and sang a song, composed by a local bard, a few lines of which translated roughly as follows:

> *Centuries of suffering,*
> *Dikes breached, the earth flooded.*
> *We were birds with clipped wings,*
> *Boats without rudders.*

> *Now rice and jute cover the fields,*
> *Green as far as the eye can see.*
> *Golden bananas, perfumed longans,*
> *Happiness smiles o'er the land.*

We dropped in at Phan hamlet of Huang Giao village, considered by Quynh as representative of new trends in the province. There had been a slaughtering of carp, chicken and pig—not to mention the greatest delicacy of all, a six-month-old puppy—to celebrate our arrival. Innumerable bottles of shumshum, the potent rice alcohol brewed in the villages, decorated the table. I was welcomed as an old friend, having visited the hamlet three years previously. Cadres from hamlet and village were there to report on recent progress. The main thing was that Phan had fused with three other co-ops as part of a general consolidation plan, which Quynh hoped would reduce to about 300 the present 800 co-ops in the province, less than two per village. This corresponded with the leveling out of the land and the creation of single fields of 20 or 30 hectares, in place of 50 or so of half a hectare each. The new co-op now included over 400 households, instead of the original 66, and covered 250 hectares served by three electric pumps. The co-op chairman, a lean, quiet man who remained very much in the background until invited to give a report, told us that the yield of rice per hectare had increased from 4,185 kilograms in 1962, when Phan was a small co-op, to 4,466 in 1965, on the big, fused, co-op.

The 1965 harvest was 46 tons higher than the combined harvests of the four smaller co-ops in 1964 because not only was the per-hectare yield somewhat higher but the area sown was greater, due to the leveling of the fields and the elimination of high and dry spots. Also because of irrigation, two crops could be harvested over the whole area instead of on only 30 per cent as previously. Sales to the state had risen from 243 tons by the four individual co-ops in 1962 to 347 tons in 1965, the increase over 1964 being 63 tons. Interesting was the fact that after a generous distribution to the co-op members, 48 tons had been put into stock. The fact that the increased tonnage sold to the state was 15 tons above the actual harvest increase was due, Quynh explained, to "austerity and patriotism."

"After all," he said, "the members know it's going to feed their husbands and sons now on the various war and construction fronts."

The chairman considered that all households of the hamlet of Phan had now reached the living standards of the former middle peasants. When I asked how this was measured, he said: "Of our 66 houses 32 are now of brick with tiled roofs, the other 34 are also brick, with thatch roofs, because there are no more tiles available at present. Poor and landless peasants lived in huts and holes in the ground before. It is the dream of every peasant everywhere in our country to have a brick house with a tiled roof. (The latter is very important, as the thatch roofs tend to be carried away during the frequent typhoons which strike just at the season when there is no rice straw to replace them.) All the courtyards are now paved with brick. The average income per head is 14 dong which we consider just above the average of the former middle peasants. Every family has proper beds, including a spare one for guests, mosquito nets, blankets and thermos flasks. Everyone has a spare set of clothes for special occasions. In the old days husband and wife sometimes shared a single pair of pants and children went naked. All that need them, and some that do not, have bicycles." When I asked what the "some that do not" meant, the chairman smiled and said: "Some parents that have young children buy a bike and tie it up under the roof, until one of the children is big enough to ride it."

When I asked about the number of working co-op members in relation to the total number of mouths to feed, the answer was revealing: The 400-odd families totalled 2,300 persons, of whom just under 600 were working members, 250 being too old to work and 1,500 too young. Each working member had to support himself and three others on the average. The labor force was split up into 16 work brigades of 20 to 25 families each and every brigade had one nurse and one midwife attached. Minister Pham Ngoc Thach's medical service was really down to the rice-roots level in the countryside. As to the campaign for toilets and the like, the chairman said the shortage of bricks and cement was holding things up: "Every three households have brick or cement-lined wells and one in every four have the closed double-toilet system. But everyone wants them and everyone can pay for them. It is a question of raw materials."

One thing that struck me in all the villages were the neat brick-paved paths leading into them and the bricked footpaths which kept down the dust and mud to manageable proportions. When I remarked on this it was explained that in this part of the country it is the custom for a young couple when they marry to add a certain yardage to the brick paths in the bridegroom's village. It is a matter of prestige to lay down the maximum possible.

As for vaccinations and inoculations against communicable diseases this was 100 per cent, it being obligatory for school children to carry certificates to this effect.

The situation in education corresponded almost exactly to that outlined at the Ministry. First-cycle schools had been relocated at co-op level, in this case at the level of the original four co-ops, but were larger than those in the bombed areas. There were eight classes of first-cycle with 344 pupils; eight of second-cycle with 316 pupils in Huang Giao village My Hao; and one class of third-cycle with 26 pupils in the district center.

Four third-cycle graduates were studying at Hanoi University, six would be admitted to the university for the 1966–67 scholastic year and three were pursuing higher studies abroad. Forty-five second-cycle graduates were studying at a technical high school. All of which one could consider not bad for a village almost entirely illiterate 12 years previously. This appeared to be encouraging confirmation that the technical revolution in the countryside would not remain a slogan and that the educational base was being prepared for a real leap ahead.

As for crime, "we have had none at all since the end of the war," said the co-op chairman. "Before, every house was surrounded by a fence, gates and doors were padlocked, but there were always thefts. In those days, the people were divided against themselves, poverty was extreme, it was reckoned that one in every three was a beggar for at least part of the year. Now there are no more fences, no padlocks and no thefts at all. If someone is in need and is embarrassed to make his needs known, the community itself notes this and helps. Everyone knows they have the co-op behind them in case of difficulties."

The conversation took place during a long and bountiful meal in the home of a 67-year-old woman, Mrs. Tuat, whose wrinkled, almost toothless face radiated goodness and kindliness. As a village elder, she had been my hostess, as far as a meeting place was concerned, on my previous visit. I asked what she thought about things now: "Since the co-op was formed and then enlarged, life has greatly changed," she said. "There are new houses everywhere. Before, when hard times came, we had to quit the village, always on the move looking for work, trying to earn a few sous. Half the time we starved. I had six children. One of them I had to give away in the old days. Impossible for my two sons, let alone my daughters, to learn to read and write. Now one of them is chief of a production brigade, the other is an expert at the Ha Bac phosphate plant. One of my daughters is a midwife, the other two are married and their husbands have proper jobs. Life is stable. I have 12 grandchildren and they will all grow up and go to school. They might become schoolteachers or engineers."

She reminded me of the old-type wooden and thatch house where she had previously received me and pointed with pride to the clean, whitewashed walls, the solid beams and tiled roof of the new brick house which she now owned. As a "soldier's mother" who had rendered great service to people like Quynh and other militants during the resistance, the first of the new homes built in Phan had been allotted to her.

The Vietnamese are a nation of poets and before we left the table one of the girls who had been helping with the meal chanted a poem in praise of My Hao district, of which the co-op was part. Situated in the north of the province, My Hao had been a chronic drought area.

> *Despite oppression and suffering,*
> *My Hao never bowed its head,*
> *But always hunted down the enemy.*
>
> *Army and people united, then and now as one,*
> *Then against the enemy,*
> *Now to reconstruct the country.*

We transform our fields in riches;
Plenitude, fertility abounds.
So rich the earth today.

Before nothing but drought,
Never a drop of water.
The peasants of My Hao never yielded to difficulties.

Now we oblige the river to flow where we want.
Sixteen square meters of earth moved
By each of everyone lending a hand.

Everyone on the job
Of strengthening the dikes.
Against the bombs and the flood.

Behold the paddy, the fine sweet potatoes,
Look at the fish amusing themselves,
Listen to the waters that sing.

And the chickens, the pigs,
That adorn all our tables,
We live better than the old, middle peasants.

What beautiful landscapes,
Flowering landscapes,
My Hao famous everywhere now.

At Van Phu village, I found Ngo Thi Thinh, former young woman chairman of a hamlet co-op when I was last there and whom I remembered for the efficient, organized way in which she had presented her report. In the intervening years she had married and become chairman of another enlarged co-op also in My Hao district. A calm, serious young woman, like so many of the peasant girls she had matured quickly once entrusted with responsibilities. The new co-op had 160 households with 644 inhabitants instead of the 34 households at her former hamlet. Of the 171 working members, 125 were women and girls. The harvest for 1965 with the enlarged co-op had been up 40 per cent over 1964 and they had sold 16 tons instead of the previous year's 10 tons of rice to the state, after allowing 16.7 kilograms of rice per month for every head of population—

yes, including newborn babes. Together with maize and potatoes, the total was the equivalent of 20 kilograms of rice per head monthly, well above the town rations. In 1964, they had launched a big attack on the irrigation and flood-prevention front, moving 3,600 cubic meters of earth; this had been continued in 1965, 5,630 cubic meters had been shifted and the work of leveling and "bulkheading" their 45 hectares of land completed. "When you last came," Ngo Thi Thinh recalled, "we had no machines at all. Now we have our own rice-husking mill and threshing machines." I asked how the war had affected the co-op.

"If the enemy comes we will fight him and continue to produce," she said. "All our members are enrolled in the 'three readies' or 'three responsibilities.' Of the 36 heads of production brigades and teams, half are women. All our young people, without exception, are members of the self-defense unit. Despite the fact that many of our young men have left for the army and construction sites, our harvest has increased and will continue to increase, even though some of our able-bodied members are permanently at the defense stations."

The visit to Hung Yen and the talks at province, district, village and co-op level, confirmed that the situation was as outlined at the Planning Commission and the Ministries of Education and Public Health. It showed that plans were not allowed to gather dust in the archives but were applied with great diligence and energy. Where they were not completely fulfilled, as with the wells and WC's, this was because of temporary factors, such as lack of raw materials. At several of the district centers, incidentally, we saw "backyard" plants engaged in mass production of standard WC's and I have no doubt that that aspect of the "revolution" will be completed soon over the whole country. The idea of sanitation had been "sold" to the peasants, which was the main thing. The physical transformation of the fields was something at which one could only marvel. The rice fields were beginning to look like the rolling fields of wheat in Australia and one could not but speculate that all this leveling out would also lead to real mechanization in modern terms. In the drier, northern part of Hung Yen tractors were already at work in many of the fields, previously impossible when the fields were broken up into innumerable, odd-shaped fragments.

By May 1966, the irrigation network covered 73 per cent of the whole cultivatable land in North Vietnam. Another 320,000 hectares of virgin land in the mountainous areas of the north-west had been brought under cultivation during the 5-year plan, adding 27 per cent to the total arable land during that period.

Another aspect that is impressive is the permanency of progress in public health and education. The Americans may be able to destroy much that has been built up in the past 12 years; bridges, factories, dikes, buildings, machinery. They can kill many people. But they cannot bomb out of existence the fact that illiteracy is a thing of the past, that hundreds of thousands of people in the villages have completed seven years of education, and millions more have completed at least four years of general education. One in three of the whole population is studying something or other, preparing to master new techniques and new machines when they become available. Not only are notions of hygiene and public health solidly implanted among the population at village and hamlet level, but there are devoted, educated medical personnel on the spot to apply them. These are considerable achievements that have not been and cannot be matched in the South, despite the billions of dollars the Americans have poured in. Without stability of government and confidence in government, it would have been impossible to achieve a fraction of what has been done in the countryside in the North, whether in flood control or the installations of Thach's double-toilet systems. The real revolution has been in the minds of the peasants, now turned outward to the world beyond their village and provincial frontiers, minds wide open to modern ideas, from family planning to chemical fertilizers and tractor-drawn ploughs. If the minds of their sons are also wide open for supersonic fighters, radar-controlled anti-aircraft guns and ground-to-air missiles, then Washington can take the credit.

Chapter 9

A SOLDIER'S VIEW

When North Vietnam's leaders speak of a war of ten, 15, or 20 or more years, the words ring less harshly on Vietnamese ears than on those of westerners. The Vietnamese, even when most of them were illiterate, have had fairly complete notions of their own history and traditions. These have been kept alive in poetry and legends and entered into the national blood-stream. In several areas of the North, for instance, where there are fantastic-shaped rocks, you can be sure that one will always be singled out by the people as representing the faithful wife, awaiting her husband's return from the war.

The theme recurs in the country's two greatest epic poems. The periodic uprisings against the Chinese during the first millennium of our era, from the heroic episode of the Trung sisters in 40 A.D. until Ngo Quyen decisively defeated the southern Hans just 900 years later in another epic battle on the Bach Dang river, are immortalized in verse and song, chanted by bards throughout the centuries. The great battles waged against the Chinese in the 11th century and the Mongols two centuries later form innumerable themes in traditional theater and opera. In more modern times the struggles against the Chinese feudalists and the Mongols formed the texts for political theses to stimulate the nation to fight against the Japanese and French. The "long war," with the whole nation engaged in repulsing the foreign invader, is part of the concept of what is considered one of the proudest of the national virtues.

In mid-1947, a series of articles written by Truong Chinh, published as a booklet under the title *The Resistance Will Win,* laid down the modern principles for the "long war." They are still considered valid today. Truong Chinh is one of the "great four" among the veteran founders of the Communist Party of Indochina and its armed forces, the others being Ho Chi Minh, Vo Nguyen Giap and Pham Van Dong. For a long time he was secretary-general of the Vietnamese Lao Dong party, formed after the formal dissolution of the CP of Indochina. He is still regarded as one of Vietnam's leading political theorists. The articles were written to stimulate and arouse confidence in the resistance war against the French which in 1947 was getting really "hot." Truong Chinh warned that the war would be long, but that victory was sure.

"To reach that point, victory, a long fight is necessary. We need time. But time works for us. Our most brilliant strategy is to be resolved to carry the resistance through to the end.

"Under the Tran (a 13th century dynasty whose Tran Hung Dao is considered one of the most brilliant of Vietnamese generals) three times in 31 years, we were obliged to wage a long resistance to beat the Mongol hordes. Under the Later Le (a 15th century dynasty) it was only after ten years of resistance that we were able to repulse the bloodthirsty Ming (Chinese) troops. The Chinese people needed eight years to rid themselves of the Japanese yoke. These examples are eloquent." Then he went on to lay down the principles on which the anti-French war was to be fought.

Those Americans who do not support their country's involvement in Vietnam—and even many who do—could draw comfort from the following lines at the start of Truong Chinh's work: "We are not waging war with France, a democratic nation which, in its new Constitution, has undertaken the following engagement:

" 'It will never undertake any war of conquest and will never employ its armed forces against the liberty of any people.'

"Are we waging war against the people of France? Again no, for the people of France, who have as their motto 'Liberty, Equality, Fraternity' do not want to wage a war of reconquest which will result in their sons being massacred for a handful of capitalists sharks. . . . We wage our war only against the French ultra-colonialists."

It is with this same spirit that today Vietnamese always refer to their enemy as "American imperialists" to stress that they have no quarrel with the USA of democratic traditions. Ho Chi Minh incorporated portions of the French and American Constitutions in the Vietnamese Constitution adopted in September 1945.

One of Vietnam's leaders summed up his country's history for me in these terms: "It has always been our fate to defend ourselves against enemies vastly superior in numbers, equipment and technique. We have had to develop strategies and tactics accordingly. Above all, we must never be in a hurry. It is the same today against the Americans."

Another thing that astonishes, and troubles, many western friends of Vietnam is the equanimity with which the Vietnamese leaders appear to contemplate the destruction of Hanoi, Haiphong and other centers and their insistence that this could have no effect on the outcome of the war. For the Vietnamese people, however, this also is not strange. In Truong Chinh's work one comes across the following passage, under the sub-title "Scorched Earth":

"Everything the enemy can turn against us, everything that we cannot retain in our own hands, we will burn, we will destroy. This is the principle of resistance by 'scorched earth.' This tactic is not a Vietnamese innovation, but the scale on which we practice it has stupified many people. Many strangers consider it mad on our part to have voluntarily razed so many towns and population centers, and burned down not only the enemy's cantonments and barracks, but have burned our own homes with our own hands. No, the Vietnamese people are not mad. If we employ the 'scorched earth' policy to a degree to which one can find few such examples in history, it is because...."

And Truong Chinh detailed the reasons that applied to the type of war the Vietnamese were then fighting and which has little to do with today's war in the North—not yet, at least. The point is, however, that then, as today, the idea that the destruction of the towns represented in itself an irreparable catastrophe is rejected. Specifically, today the idea (which Washington seemed to entertain at one period) that the threat of destroying Hanoi and Haiphong would bring Ho Chi Minh to the conference table on Washington's terms, betrays a desperate ignorance of Vietnamese sentiments and traditions. If the Vietnamese people in the first resistance were prepared to burn their own towns and set fire to their homes with their own hands, they are not likely to fall to their knees because the enemy destroys their towns and homes or threatens to do so.

On the question of whether the North Vietnamese are serious when they speak of a "long war," the complete transformation of the country's economic and social life is answer enough. As to whether the struggle continues or Ho Chi Minh runs to the conference table wringing his hands because Hanoi and Haiphong are bombed, one can only hope that Washington will not put the matter to the test. That Hanoi and Haiphong will be defended as efficiently as possible there is no doubt; radical measures have been taken to ensure that civilian losses will be minimal, and also damage to economic potentials. But the strategy of "preparing for the worst" above all takes into account that Hanoi and Haiphong will be bombed and even that attempts will be made to breach the Red River dikes. The North Vietnamese leaders do not believe that any moral, legal or humanitarian considerations will restrain Washington's hands in this. They do believe, however, that the cost of such a venture could be a restraining factor and that an aroused, articulate world public opinion still more so.

However, whether the doctrine of the "long war" still remains valid, in view of the tremendous destructive capacity of American air power, was a subject worthy of discussion with Vietnam's No. 1 soldier, General Vo Nguyen Giap. The former Saigon history teacher built up the Vietnam People's Army from a ragged ill-armed platoon into the formidable machine that carried off the historic victory of Dien Bien Phu and he took on and beat one after another France's most brilliant generals and marshals. I found him in excellent form. He had lost a few pounds in weight and ten years in age since I had last met him, two years previously. Exuding confidence and energy, he had abandoned the formal bemedaled uniform he usually wears on such occasions for an open-necked khaki shirt, more befitting his reactivated role. And he was very much the man of action again, dealing every hour with matters that he understood at least as well as any of his profession in the world today.

The interview was to be filmed and recorded for the TV, and General Giap was quietly amused as Roger Pic, the French TV producer who was personally filming the interview, directed him how to sit in relation to the microphone, shouting out very uninhibitedly instructions from the camera: "Shoulder a little higher, face more toward the camera, further back from the microphone." We were sitting in the garden in the grounds of the Defense Ministry, aides standing around, scandalized at the shouted instructions. Giap chuckled and moved obediently. "I'm the one who usually gives orders around here," he said. "Go ahead," he shouted back to Pic, "you're in charge today." The questions and answers were as follows:

"From the military viewpoint, how do you evaluate the results of 15 months of American air attacks against the DRV?"

"As you know, in carrying out their attacks and bombardments against the DRV, at the same time as the intensification of their aggression in South Vietnam, the Americans aimed at breaking the morale of our people, at destroying our military and economic potential and, thus, at changing the situation in South Vietnam in their favor.

"Ever since their defeat in Korea and after the first setbacks for the GI's in South Vietnam, the Americans have had a glimpse of what is involved for them in committing American infantry on the Asian mainland. And, in passing, they still went into it with their eyes open. So much the worse for them! Also, the idea of waging war with their air force against the DRV seemed a happy brain-wave at first. In order to carry it out they mobilized their planes from the Seventh Fleet as well as squadrons based in South Vietnam and Thailand. They have indiscriminately attacked communications and industrial centers and populated areas in North Vietnam, not sparing even crèches, schools, hospitals, pagodas and churches.

"The Americans have not, however, attained their goals. Their open and cynical aggression against the DRV, an independent and sovereign country, a member of the socialist camp, has only stirred up hatred and reinforced the Vietnamese people's will to fight, and provoked a vast movement throughout the world, including in the United States itself. Even the Pentagon has been forced to admit that it is dealing with an adversary who shows not the slightest sign of weakness.

"Our army and our people have inflicted heavy losses on the enemy. Till this day (it was April 24, 1966), 967 enemy planes have been downed. And the construction of socialism continues.

We had a marvellous harvest last year. As you've been able to see for yourself, the railway is still running, prices have not increased. Our military and economic potential has increased, not diminished.

"And how have things gone in South Vietnam? Our compatriots have wiped out some of the best American units in Zone D, north of Saigon, at Plei Me, at Ia Drang, in the coastal plains of Central Vietnam. They have successfully attacked such solidly defended bases as Danang, Chu Lai, Bien Hoa and quite recently at Tan Son Nhat (Saigon airport). The South Vietnamese mercenary army has suffered a series of defeats. As for the Saigon puppet government which President Johnson at Honolulu did everything possible to pull off the rocks, what does it govern today? The political events at present taking place at Danang, Hue, Saigon and in other towns of South Vietnam,* show it doesn't even control the urban centers. On the other hand, the South Vietnam Liberation Army has shown its mettle; it is capable of beating the American and other forces no matter how well armed they are. The National Liberation Front has once again proven that it is the only authentic representative of the South Vietnamese people.

"Things are clear. The 15 months of aerial bombardments against the DRV have resulted in further heavy defeats for the American aggressors, in North as in South Vietnam. Add to this their extremely serious political isolation. Today, more than ever before, they are in an impasse." And the general smiled a very satisfied smile.

"In the past few days," I said, "the Americans have employed B-52's against the North. They have also bombarded Nam Dinh and the outskirts of Hanoi and Haiphong, the three biggest cities of the North. What do you think about this?"

"These savage bombing raids are no surprise to us," replied

* The interview took place during the upheaval in Central Vietnam when students and Buddhists, supported by elements of Saigon's armed forces, seized control of Danang and Hue. The dismissal by Saigon Premier Nguyen Cao Ky of General Thi, commander of the First Military Zone which includes Danang and Hue, was the ostensible reason for the revolt which was supported by Buddhists and students in Saigon.

General Giap. "They express the hysterical American reaction to the new military and political reverses in South Vietnam. Far from halting the deterioration of their situation in the South and raising the morale of the handful of despicable agents, all they have done is to once more unmask the impudent trickery involved in the Johnson Administration's so-called proposals for 'unconditional negotiations.' The American government will itself be to blame for the serious consequences of each new military adventure against the DRV."

"What is your reaction to one of the American theses according to which they can win the war in South Vietnam by paralyzing the port of Haiphong and, in general, destroying the economic potential of your country?" I wanted to know.

Giap laughed: "It is not theses that are lacking for the American strategists. There are the theses you speak about, but there are also other, more reasonable ones which affirm that it is in South Vietnam itself that the outcome of the war will be decided.

"The only correct thesis, in fact, is this: The war which the US Government is waging in South Vietnam is an aggressive war, a neo-colonial war of aggression. As for our people in South Vietnam, they are fighting in legitimate defense, to safeguard their national rights and to contribute to peace in Asia and the world. Strong in their own right, united as one man, knowing how to wield the invincible weapon of people's war, supported by the socialist countries and peace and justice-loving people all over the world, they are going from success to success—even after the air attacks were launched against the DRV.

"Whatever methods the Americans employ, or may employ, they will never be able to change this irreversible truth in our present-day epoch, the age of the triumph of socialism and people's liberation movements. Our liberation war is a just one. We will win."

General Giap spoke very forcefully at this point and it was to be noted that he stressed "our" liberation war and "we" will win, which implied that the struggle in the South was also very much the struggle of the North and it was with this in mind that I posed the next question.

"What, according to you, will be the results if the Americans attack at the same time both North and South Vietnam?"

"Vietnam is one, it is indivisible. The 1954 Geneva Agreements expressly provided for its reunification by peaceful means. Intervention, followed by armed aggression by the Americans in the South, already constitutes a very grave violation of our country's sovereignty. By their air raids against the DRV, they have carried the war to the whole of Vietnam. In such circumstances . . ." (and Giap was about to start smiting the table, had not an abrupt signal from Pic, worried about the effects on the microphone, arrested his fist, in mid-air, but his words were very forceful again) ". . . We will resist American aggression, arms in hand, for our national salvation is the most sacred duty of every Vietnamese patriot, of the entire Vietnamese people. Our people are determined to fight to defend the North, to liberate the South and to achieve the peaceful reunification of the Motherland."

"How then do you envisage the evolution of the war in the South and in North Vietnam?"

"The American war of aggression against Vietnam will continue to develop as it has developed until now. It will go from reverse to reverse until it ends in total defeat. But our people's liberation war will go from success to success to end in final victory.

"As everyone now knows, the USA experimented with their neo-colonial policy by installing the sanguinary regime of Ngo Dinh Diem with the use of 150,000 Diemist troops equipped and supported by Washington. And they failed lamentably.

"After that it was the famous 'special war' which Kennedy launched and which Johnson continued with half a million South Vietnamese mercenaries and some 30,000 American 'advisers.' In its turn, 'special war' also failed while the heroic people of South Vietnam brought off ever bigger successes.

"Now it is again a new stage. Washington has sent a massive American expeditionary corps, comprising elite troops, and they are waging an 'escalation' war against North Vietnam. But has the military and political situation of the USA in Vietnam improved with all this? Absolutely not. On the contrary, it has rapidly worsened. The Americans have failed in what they called their 'dry season' offensive. They will fail again. They have failed in their desperate attempt to stabilize the Saigon puppet government. However, the liberation armed forces and the people of South Vietnam have brought off more and more striking victories and the DRV still remains solid, stronger than ever.

"The Americans can reinforce their expeditionary crops in South Vietnam. They can intensify their air bombardment of North Vietnam, even engage in other adventurous measures. But the further they get involved in the war, the more they will expose themselves to heavy defeats.

"Our country has been at war for over 20 years. Our people deeply desire peace. But as our President Ho Chi Minh has said, 'There is no true peace without true independence.' We will fight until final victory against the American aggressors, to safeguard the independence of our country, to realize the profound aspirations of our people for liberty and reunification, to contribute to the maintenance of peace in Asia and throughout the world. *We will win.*"

And as the interview was primarily intended for French TV viewers, General Giap concluded by addressing a few words to the French people, whom he said "were always at our side, and actively support our just struggle against American aggression" —a support for which he expressed "sincere thanks," on behalf of the Vietnamese people.

General Giap obviously did not intend to get involved in any details as to the extent that the North was helping the South; had he thought this desirable he could have risen to the bait of my question as to the results of the Americans' creating a single military front by "attacking at the same time both North and South Vietnam," but the implication of this reply was clear.

In this connection it is worthwhile recalling that when the National Liberation Front of South Vietnam held its First Congress (February 16–March 3, 1962) to draw up a Constitution, a Declaration was issued in which the Front warned as to the consequences of further direct US intervention:

"Congress affirms that if . . . the US imperialists and their agents plunge deeper into their bloodthirsty aggression . . . the people of South Vietnam and the National Liberation Front

will use all forms of struggle, will take all measures to fight
resolutely in order to save themselves and their country—to
liberate South Vietnam, to defend independence and democracy,
and completely overthrow treacherous dictators. In case of necessity, the people of South Vietnam and the NLF will use their
legitimate and effective right to *appeal to the people and the
government of North Vietnam,* to peace-loving and democratic
peoples and governments the world over, irrespective of political systems, *requesting that active support, including material and manpower support,* be afforded to the just struggle of
the South Vietnamese people. US imperialists and their agents
must bear the full responsibility for any disastrous consequences." (Emphasis added.)

As a corollary to that, when the American government decided in mid-1965 to send another 50,000 troops to South Vietnam, the Central Committee of the NLF on August 3, 1965, issued an appeal which included the following:

"We launch a fraternal appeal to the army and people of the
North to actively accord, in every way, their help to the South
Vietnamese people, thus enabling us to reinforce our armed
forces and push ahead with our resistance for the independence
of the Motherland.

"We appeal to those inhabitants and soldiers of the South,
who are installed in the North, to regroup in units and to be
prepared to regain the South to fight against the US imperialists
and to save their country and their families.

"We invite the Indochinese people *to unite and help each
other* to resist the brutal US aggression and that of their puppets, to defend their independence and at the same time to defend the common peace of the countries of Indochina, of Southeast Asia and of the entire world . . . !"

In connection with the second paragraph it must be recalled
that some 140,000 South Vietnamese, mainly members of the
regular Vietminh army, were withdrawn from South Vietnam
and regrouped in the North after the Geneva Agreements, in
compliance with provisions to separate the combatants. French
and allied forces in the North were likewise regrouped and
withdrawn to the South. This withdrawal was intended, as far
as the Vietminh units were concerned, as a temporary measure,

pending the reunification of the country by general elections in July 1956 as provided by Geneva. The elections did not take place, the regroupees stayed in the North, chafing at their in-action during the great repression against former resistance members by the Diem regime, which inevitably hit first and hardest at the families of the regroupees. It is hardly likely that the "army and people of the North" would refuse the Libera-tion Front's appeal or that the regroupees would not jump at the chance to get into uniforms again (in case they had ever taken them off) and start off for the South with guns in hand and a burning thirst for revenge in their hearts. Or that the Pathet Lao, which controlled almost the entire Laotian border with South Vietnam, would have been slow to an appeal to "unite and help each other." It is curious that the Front appeal seemed to pass unnoticed by western news agencies in Saigon which monitor Liberation Radio.

Whether northern troops of the regular Vietnam People's Army are in action in the South is another question. It hardly seems necessary. Of the 140,000 regroupees, moved to the North in 1954–55, a few were wives and children but the overwhelm-ing proportion were troops and political cadres. The total of troops claimed by the Americans as having "infiltrated" from the North to the South by May 1966 was in the region of 30,000, so a great deal more "infiltration" would have to take place be-fore the 100,000 or so authentic southern troops come back home. Just as they came from the South, most of them in regu-lar units, so the NFL appealed to them to return as regular units. There was nothing, incidentally, in the Geneva Agree-ments that required them to demobilize after arriving in the North, or which banned them being trained in the use of more sophisticated weapons. Nor was there anything in the Geneva Agreements that suggested they should remain permanently in the North. On the contrary, it was expressly stated and im-plicit in the Agreements that regrouping was purely a tempo-rary device to permit the separation of combatants. In fact, many of the units that came from the South did demobilize, but they remained together, very often on state farms in the frontier areas, where they settled down in battalion and regimental-sized units, got married, raised children, and started to produce coffee, rubber, and rice, the rank-and-file continuing their military training as local self-defense units. The officers went off to annual refresher courses to keep themselves abreast of modern military techniques.

To what extent the North helps the South, and in what form, are military secrets, but for several years after the armed struggle started in the South, I believe, there was no help. This was a source of great national frustration to the North Vietnamese, as I felt particularly in visits to the North in 1963 and 1964. Many responsible cadres in the North will argue privately (although this is never said publicly) that by attacking the North, the Americans in fact abolished the 17th parallel. They say that as the North is being bombed to bits for allegedly aiding the South, there is no reason not to go ahead and to do what they are being punished for; and, further, as the air attacks are partly mounted from bases in the South, the DRV is perfectly justified under any definition of international law to send its army south to try and wipe out those bases and to overthrow the government that permits the use of such bases. Who has more right to be in South Vietnam anyway, they ask, Americans, Koreans, Australians, New Zealanders—or Vietnamese even if they do come from north of a provisional demarcation line?

Everyone I met in Hanoi knows the North is now helping the South and rejoices in the fact, even though they may not know in exactly what form. The feeling of national frustration has disappeared. "Defend the North and Liberate the South" has become a national slogan. Also there was no doubt in the minds of any with whom I spoke that arms will not be laid down until the country is reunified. It is considered that it was the Americans who threw down the challenge by starting the bombings.

Whether the North was actually helping the South at the time of the first bombings, and if so to what extent, is a subject no one will discuss in the North. But it is pointed out that aid to the South was not the original American pretext for the first bombings against Dong Hoi in February 1965. The official reason was that these were "retaliatory" raids for a "Vietcong" attack against an American airfield at Pleiku. Later, as the raids continued, the official pretext was that they were aimed at getting Hanoi to the conference table. Finally, after the happy discovery of an arms cache on the coast of Central Vietnam, the pretext was "stabilized"—the bombings were aimed at cutting off infiltration of men and arms from the North.

The New York Times in an editorial on May 20, 1966, incidentally exposed the hollowness of all the pretexts for the bombings. It said: "In the summer of 1964 Premier Khanh was promised a bombing offensive against the North, presumably on presidential authority, to extract pledges from Saigon of governmental stability and efficacy. When the bombing of the North finally began the following winter, its primary objective—as explained by the highest American officials in Saigon—was to stabilize the politics of South Vietnam."

It is worth noting that President Johnson seems to have privately given this pledge to the Saigon government at the moment that he was publicly attacking Senator Goldwater for suggesting that North Vietnam should be bombed. The idea that Saigon was to be stabilized by bombing the North seems as sterile, 15 months afterward, as the idea that the war in the South can be won by "smashing the North" or by destroying Hanoi and Haiphong.

Writing from Saigon in the *Herald Tribune* (European edition, Nov. 23, 1965), correspondent Jack Foisie noted that "even airmen concede that nine months of bombing the routes of North Vietnam does not seriously interfere with the Asian way of travel—by foot, sampan and oxcart." He went on to report: "There are indications that Hanoi began to prepare for this confrontation with US units as early as May, *soon after the first US Marines landed.* In May and June the first North Vietnamese units now are known to have crossed into South Vietnam. At this stage, it appears that the US escalation of the ground war had been answered by Hanoi with an escalation of its own (emphasis added)." In other words, according to Foisie, North Vietnam's intervention was the *reaction* to American bombings in the North (which had started in February) and the commitment of US combat troops in the South, and not the *cause* of the bombings and intervention. But this revelation does not prevent Foisie from reporting in the same article that the two US bombing objectives were "to strike the routes of infiltration and slow the entry of the North Vietnamese," which it was apparently calculated would follow the initial bombings, and "to confront Hanoi with a sample of US military strength and thus encourage peace talks." Pretexts are used, in fact, to justify a certain stage in "escalation" and then thrown on the scrapheap, the authors counting on the public's notoriously short memory. Foisie admits that neither of the objectives had been achieved and quotes those advocating further "escalation" as noting that "in addition to the factories around Hanoi and the port of Haiphong, the dikes of the Red River have never been attacked. If the dikes were breached, the rice-growing delta would be inundated during certain seasons of the year." Foisie also refers to "the belief that Hanoi is putting more and more of its own regular troops into the war to add a talking point should negotiations occur. 'It will be a remove-your-American-troops and we'll-remove-ours sort of argument' one source said."

This is another example of the woeful ignorance of American policy-makers and their spokesmen in Saigon and Washington! Whatever Vietnamese troops are now fighting in South Vietnam are there to stay. Any troops that may have come from the North—or returned from the North, which is the more likely proposition—are under the centralized command of the Liberation Army of South Vietnam. They will never be withdrawn. There will never be another settlement based on a "regroupment" to the North. In that sense also the Americans have bombed the 17th parallel to smithereens. These points, at least, were among those made in conversations I have had with responsible policy-makers in the North and in the Liberation Front areas in the South. Americans have to withdraw, not Vietnamese.

Until this happens the war will continue, even for many more years, even at the cost of Hanoi and Haiphong being destroyed and the Red River dikes being breached. When Ho Chi Minh says "We will fight ten, 15, 20 or more years, we will win," the Vietnamese people do not consider this a "pep talk." They take such utterances as solemn statements of fact, a program of action. By all one could see, hear and feel, they accept without question that their lives and activities will be directed to that end. But it is doubtful if Washington's CIA and the Pentagon computers are capable of absorbing facts as simple as these.

Chapter 10

HANOI COMPUTERS

Washington, more specifically the Pentagon, is known to rely heavily on computers these days in deciding Vietnam war policies and strategies. Hanoi also has its computers, continuously pitted against those of Washington. History will doubtless have rich comment on the relative efficiency of the two systems, as shown by the battlefield and conference table results. Off-hand, Hanoi would not seem to have much chance in such an unequal test. However, a Hanoi computer which so far has consistently turned up a high percentage of right answers is General Nguyen Van Vinh, the brilliant assistant chief-of-staff of the Vietnam People's Army. For years past he has also been chairman of the Committee for Reunification, a body set up immediately after the Geneva Agreements to prepare the various steps toward reunification as it was conceived those days. Foreign observers in Hanoi consider General Vinh an outstanding military theoretician. So do the Vietnamese.

Since 1962 I have had the benefit of several long sessions with General Vinh in which he gave his estimate of how the war in the South would develop. They were all notable for his uncanny perception of American intentions, strategies and tactics and how they would be foiled. General Vinh, very tall for a Vietnamese, slim, with a lean, clever face, crinkly dark hair and an acutely shy manner, gave me an analysis in 1962, for instance, of General Maxwell Taylor's brainchild, "special war," explaining how it would be applied in Vietnam and how it would be defeated. He also gave a comprehensive analysis of "special war" in relation to America's global commitments and the possibility of it later developing into "limited war" in South Vietnam (that is, the commitment of American combat troops instead of the tele-guided war based on South Vietnamese troops with American "advisers"). These analyses and predictions were correct, even down to numbers of troops that would be engaged and approximate dates, the development of the military-political counter-attacks which would, and did, defeat "special war" in the South. In this, General Vinh showed superiority over the Pentagon computers which had advised Defense Secretary Mc-Namara that he could count on a "special war" victory by the end of 1965 and withdraw all US military "advisers" by then, as McNamara believed and announced. Actually, US troops increased from about 20,000 to 180,000 between the beginning and end of 1965.

Because of his past accuracy, I was all the more eager to hear computer Vinh's view on the perspectives now that the USA was getting ever more involved in "limited war" in South Vietnam and in all-out air war in the North.

On his table General Vinh had a copy of an article on just this subject, which he had written for the VPA theoretical journal. The first point he made was that no matter how many troops the USA put into South Vietnam, they would not be able to change the balance of forces in their favor. According to original US estimates, a superiority of 10 or 15 to one in their favor was necessary to win in a guerrilla war. As this was manifestly impossible to achieve they had scaled the ratio down to five to one, but this would also be impossible to achieve. The Liberation Army could be reinforced quickly enough and the Saigon forces destroyed quickly enough to constantly change the relationship of forces in favor of the Liberation Front, even if the USA put in 300,000 or 400,000 or more troops. The massive commitment of US forces since May 1965 had proved this, despite the scale and the speed of the build-up to nearly 250,-000 troops. Whatever change in the relationship of forces had taken place, it had been in favor of the Liberation Front.

"The forces that a country can deploy in a war," said General Vinh, "include the following factors: the number and morale of troops that can be sent to the front line; support from military allies and other non-belligerent friendly countries. If we count on only the economic war potential, the arms and technique, it is obvious that the enemy is immeasurably stronger than us. In this respect, as throughout all our history, we have to face an enemy far stronger than ourselves. But if we consider all the elements that both sides are able to throw into this specific war, in the South as well as in the country as a whole, we can conclude that we are the stronger." He listed a number of these factors on both sides, as follows:

The American position:

(1) The USA was engaged in a war far from American shores and remote from the country's vital interests. It was an unpopular war at home and among America's allies. It was clearly an unjust war.

(2) Although the USA was immeasurably stronger in men and materials than Vietnam, she was obliged to cope with hostile, or potentially hostile, situations in many parts of the world and could not focus her entire strength on Vietnam alone.

(3) The Saigon troops were almost at their last tether by the time the American troops arrived. Their units were badly under strength; their morale in ruins. Troops sent by America's allies are limited in numbers and this will continue to be so, because of their local problems, including popular opposition to the war.

(4) Because of the above factors the Americans have not been able to establish overwhelming numerical superiority on the fronts and have to rely on old-fashioned concepts based on superior arms and technique; trying to deal rapid, decisive blows and snatch a quick, military victory.

The Vietnamese position:

(*Be it noted that General Vinh spoke of the war as being waged, more or less, on a single front.*)

(1) Because it is a just war waged in defense of our soil and homes, South Vietnamese armed forces are reinforced by millions of patriots who take part in the war in thousands of different ways. If we include the three types of troops—the regular army, regional troops and local self-defense guerrillas—they are absolutely superior to the enemy in numbers and in quality.

(2) Because of support from the people and the existence of the three categories of troops, losses in any of the three categories can easily be replaced from the great manpower reserves at their disposal.

(3) The NLF rely not only on classic weapons but also on a great variety of rudimentary weapons, traps and so forth, made

from local materials, and which when used in passive defense of villages cause numerous losses to the enemy.

(4) Patriots in the South receive unstinted support from the population of the North, increasing material support from the socialist camp and moral support from all over the world, including inside the USA.

"All the above," continued General Vinh, "adds up to the fact that the South Vietnamese people are waging a revolutionary type of war, a people's war which the adversary is incapable of countering. The commitment of US combat troops in the South and the attacks against the North only increase US difficulties because for all our people it is now clear that once again our nation is face to face with a foreign invader!"

I raised the question of the great manpower reserves of the USA. Would it not be possible by sheer weight of numbers to seize and maintain the military initiative, overwhelm Liberation Front positions and gradually reoccupy the areas now controlled by the Front?

General Vinh was adamant that this would be impossible: "They cannot regain the initiative; they cannot reoccupy terrain, they cannot change the situation in any sense favorable to them."

He pointed out that the Americans, hoping to do things in a hurry, had committed their very best, elite divisions, and that although the Vietnamese considered these of very low quality, it was still the best the Americans had. He noted discussion in the US press expressing alarm that the "elite" troops from America's only well-trained divisions would be pulled out after having completed their 12-month combat duty, and speculating with considerable gloom as to how their green replacements would fare.

"The Americans themselves admit that these are their best troops," said General Vinh, "But what have they to show after a year's fighting? Nothing."

General Vo Nguyen Giap, in conversation after the TV interview, had described as "pitiful" the quality of the "veterans" of the 1st Infantry and 1st Airmobile divisions. "By all the accounts we receive," he said, "they are greenhorns, not to be compared with the French, in their time. They have no idea of jungle fighting or guerrilla warfare and they're up against the most experienced guerrillas in the world. They walk into traps that wouldn't fool a baby and are massacred by the scores and hundreds. And now they're starting to send real schoolboys."

Now, Nguyen Van Vinh drew a comparison with the Korean war, where the US and allied forces had a total of some 400,000-odd troops, all of which, because of a stable rear, could be concentrated along the battleline, opposite the North Korean-Chinese forces. Even half a million troops in South Vietnam, he believed, would be powerless to handle the revolutionary movement there. "They have no stable rear and the front is everywhere," he said. "They speak glibly of the offensives through Laos. But where are they going to get the troops? What do they think we will be doing meanwhile? And the Pathet Lao?

"The crack US Marine troops in Danang, 34,000-strong, have been trying to link up with another 10,000 Marines at Chu Lai, 50-odd miles away, along comparatively level country. They've still not been able to do it after a whole year. Each time they've tried to clear the road they've badly burned their fingers. Look at their rear—even in Danang city itself! How can they dream of pushing through a couple of hundred miles of jungle and mountains in Southern Laos, holding and occupying it. That might look very attractive on the maps they print in their newspapers. Perhaps it is of comfort to the US public. But in fact they cannot do it."

I asked about the possibility of the Americans carrying the ground war to North Vietnam. The American press had carried some details of a plan drawn up in 1965 for landings along the narrow waist, just north of the 17th parallel, where there are good landing beaches, the main north-south highway runs very close to the coast and there is only about 30 miles of North Vietnamese territory between the coast and the mountains of Laos.

"Then the relations of forces would change still more to their disfavor," he said. "Tackling the North would be something very different than fighting the NLF in the South. We have very solid defenses at our disposal. The DRV is a member of the socialist camp and were it necessary, the socialist countries would come to our aid." I had been informed from another high-level source in Hanoi that China alone was ready to put in a million troops "for a start" the moment the North felt the need, and the offer was made in full expectation of American retaliation. It was doubtless with this in view that General Vinh added: "If the Americans undertook to hit the North, when the reverses are piling up in their rear in the South, then no matter what size the force they committed, they could not avoid a disastrous defeat by the immense forces of their adversaries in this region."

General Vinh then quoted a passage from his own article about the "non-existent rear" of the Americans in South Vietnam. "In any conflict when an attacker has wiped out his adversary or forced him to retreat, he usually seizes an area, installs his power there and the region is immediately transformed into his rear. Willy-nilly, the human and material resources of the region become, in whole or at least the major part, a source for replacing his losses. In numerous regions of our country however . . . despite savage measures of repression, our adversaries have never found a quiet corner to establish a foothold." He then referred to the various pacification plans, the Staley-Taylor plan, the McNamara plan, the "pacification by sector" plans and others tried out by Ambassador Maxwell Taylor and Cabot Lodge and more recently by retired Major General Lansdale. "All these efforts have been crowned with failure, even though they have employed whole divisions for a year or two to 'pacify' at any cost some districts, even two or three villages at the gates of Saigon-Cholon or the approaches to American bases.

"The guerrillas and other Liberation forces not only continue to operate on the outskirts of the enemy's key towns, but they carry out sudden and devastating blows right in the center of these towns and solidly-defended bases. At the same time, the population of the Saigon-controlled areas wages fierce struggles against measures such as taxes, levies, fines, forced relocation of villages and above all the conscription of young people into the armed forces. The enemy is absolutely unable to exploit the human and material resources even in the areas he controls. He cannot even eat or sleep in peace at his place of work or his barracks and dormitories . . . Not even in his hotels in the heart of Saigon," said General Vinh, with one of his shy smiles.

Setting aside his article, he continued: "To have such an unstable rear is contrary to all the axioms of war, especially if one contemplates a further extension of military activities." He explained the instability of the American rear as due to the "high political consciousness and deep patriotism" of the Vietnamese people. "You have travelled around our countryside in the North, slept in the villages, visited the construction sites and evacuated factories and army units," he said. "You can judge for yourself whether our rear is stable or not. You can compare that to what is published every day in the American press about the situation in the South. Military history shows that no belligerent can be considered winning if he fails to secure his rear and transform the human and material resources there to his own needs. The Americans have failed to do this, they will never be able to do it. That is another reason why their defeat is inevitable."

"Now that the Americans have committed a quarter of a million troops and are beginning to play a major, sometimes exclusive, role in military operations," I asked, "is the role of the Saigon troops still important?"

"Definitely yes," replied General Vinh. "There are still important vestiges of 'special war' in the situation. The Americans have not enough troops, and no machinery at all, to start occupying the country and administering it. It is quite different than when the French came back in 1945–46 with their old colonial apparatus, people who knew the country and were used to running an administration. That was the product of 80 years of experience. With over 230,000 troops what have the Americans succeeded in occupying? Ten or 12 of some 200 provincial capitals and district centers. They cannot garrison those centers, let alone administer the population and the surrounding countryside. They have no one who knows the country or people, nor with any experience of the type of administration needed. So they need the Saigon troops and what counts for a government. These remain an important military and political prop inside the country, and they help to maintain the fiction abroad that the USA is not playing the old, colonialist game in South Vietnam but merely helping a 'friendly government which asked for help.' Even if they could occupy the country, it would also destroy that fiction if they were to try and establish the sort of occupation regimes set up for enemy territory in Europe after the war. The Saigon troops also still serve as cannon-fodder; lots of the dirtiest and most dangerous jobs are left to them and this reduces American manpower losses. So, though the scope and nature of the war has changed, the role of the puppets is still important."

"During my second visit to the Liberation Front areas," I remarked, "when Americans were still only 'advisers,' they were 'first priority' targets. Is this now so on a wider scale? Are the American units now the priority targets for the Liberation Army?"

"That's a question you would really have to ask at Liberation Army headquarters," General Vinh replied with a smile. "But by the reports from the battle-fronts, I would say that American units and the Saigon army units both receive plenty of attention; there are no 'priorities' in that sense. As for the Saigon forces, about one third of their infantry battalions were wiped out during 1965. Five of their ten divisions (the 2nd, 22nd, 5th, 25th, and 27th) were defeated on several occasions with heavy losses, each division losing about half of their battalions. The remaining five divisions also received heavy blows. Very important for Nguyen Cao Ky and the Americans were the heavy losses inflicted on the 12 battalions of Saigon's 'strategic reserve' of parachute and marine battalions, half of which were completely wiped out. As for the provincial, district and village security forces, they have taken very heavy losses, rendering them incapable of offensive actions. They are reduced to trying to defend the provincial and district centers, for the main part digging in behind extensive fortifications.

"If the Saigon troops in Central Vietnam, including even divisional and area commanders, have suddenly turned against Saigon, this is not so much because they have suddenly begun to embrace the Buddhist leadership, but because of the crushing defeats and heavy losses they have suffered in a war that is, more clearly than ever, an American war. Another element is that the officers, who mainly come from the urban centers, are humiliated and enraged by what they know is happening to Vietnamese women, including those from their own families, in American-occupied centers. A major reason for the low combat efficiency of the Saigon regular army, apart from the low morale, is that Nguyen Cao Ky has partly replaced battle losses with troops from lower-grade units, trained only in passive defense. To be specific, the NLF attach great importance to destroying the Saigon army and depriving the Americans of this prop and shield."

"American correspondents from Saigon, with whom I have spoken, maintain that the arrival of American troops and their great array of modern equipment gave a big boost to the morale of the Saigon troops. This is still the official American position. How do you feel about that?" I asked.

"It did for a while," General Vinh conceded, "especially as the Americans started arriving at a time when the Saigon forces were in a desperate situation; their morale was so low that the whole machine was on the verge of collapse. The sight of thousands of well-built, superbly equipped American troops with landing craft, tanks, big guns and hundreds of helicopters undoubtedly boosted the morale of the high-ranking officers who saw in this invasion the salvation for their personal fortunes and even their skins. In certain cases and certain places, the US forces gave the Saigon troops useful support and got them out of tight places mainly by the use of air power. But by and large the fate of the Saigon troops remained unchanged. And they began to see that the Americans were not super-men. In fact they fell into ambushes more readily than did the Saigon troops; they couldn't move without noise and when they did move, it was at snail's pace, despite their much-vaunted mobility. They also fell when bullets hit them. The Americans also made the great mistake of forcing the pace in the mountain areas, a graveyard for French forces in the past and for the Saigon forces since the Americans arrived.

"During 1964, before the Americans arrived, less than ten battalions of Saigon troops were wiped out in these regions. But in 1965, especially after the First Airmobile Cavalry Division set up its headquarters at An Khe, almost 40 Saigon battalions were wiped out in the mountain areas. In the beginning there were cases when the Americans came to the aid of the Saigon troops, but afterwards it was more often that Saigon troops were sent to rescue the Americans, as at the Plei Me battle.

"In the plains the situation for the Saigon troops has not appreciably improved. The Americans have not been able to relieve them from their main tasks—trying to protect provincial and district towns and the few 'strategic hamlets' that remain. The American forces have their work cut out trying to defend their own bases, let alone trying to take over the defense of South Vietnamese towns. So puppet morale continues to fall and defections are very high, even from the network of strong points set up to protect Saigon and a few key centers. The very fact that the Americans themselves announced the defection of 113,-000 Saigon troops during 1965, the great year of American intervention, answers your question and the assertions in the American press.

"From the beginning Liberation Front strategy has been to wage a carefully integrated military-political struggle. The whole population takes part in day-to-day political work directed at the Saigon troops, appealing to their patriotism, awakening the old national virtues. There is no let-up in this and the Americans have nothing in their arsenal of super-weapons to counter this infallible weapon of ours." And there General Vinh probably scored one up on the Pentagon computer programmers who would probably boggle at having to find a mathematical expression for a weapon called "national virtues."

"The question which bothers many of your well-wishers around the world," I said, "is how you can believe that you can beat the Americans. Many people, including a number of experienced western correspondents, now concede that the Americans cannot win; but they also do not believe that the Liberation Front can win in the South or that you can defeat American air power in the North."

"When we speak of beating the Americans," replied General Vinh, "we have no ambitions or desires to impose a military victory over the United States as such. We want them to stop their aggression against our country in the South as in the North, and get out. That is the victory we are after. We do not want to chase them anywhere, or sink their fleets, expel them from other bases that have nothing to do with us, far less invade their territory. We fight, as we have fought throughout our history, for our national independence, for the whole of our country. When we have achieved that, we will have won.

"We have difficulty explaining things even to our closest friends," he continued with a rather tired smile, picking up his article again. "But based on what we consider a sober analysis of all the factors, we are certain we can win, certain that we can defeat every branch of American arms engaged in this war. Let us consider them one at a time. On what are the Americans counting?—a great deal on their monoply of air power. True this gives appreciable support in firepower and rapid transport of troops. But it also has its limitations.

"Let's look at B-52's for a start: Two divisions of the Strategic Air Command are engaged so far. They carry out almost daily raids on the South and have now made their appearance in the North. But if one considers the number of raids and compares the tonnage of bombs dropped with the damage caused, these are the least efficient planes in the American air arsenal. They are the least accurate in bombing and cause the least casualties. For 'extermination' raids against big cities, with high concentrations of industry and population not defended with modern weapons, they could doubtless be deadly and destructive. Against our towns in the North, they would be easy to knock down because of their size and lack of maneuverability and our sophisticated defenses. In the South, because of the low density of the rural population in the areas they are trying to hit—and the tendency is to thin out all the time—and because of well-tested defense measures by the Liberation Army troops, they are inefficient. As tactical weapons to influence ground actions, as during the Ia Drang battle, they are ludicrous. Such extreme measures used to insure that American troops will not be on the receiving end are so elaborate that the element of surprise is completely lost. To hit the NLF forces they have to risk hitting their own as well.

"About 3,000 planes of other types, including helicopters, are being used in the South and their number is increasing all the time; their main role is to give close support to infantry in ground operations, but they are also used to bomb 'hostile' areas. Against the NLF forces, they can only influence, more or less, the combat methods and the duration of an engagement, the timing of an attack and of disengagement, the manner of gaining mastery of the terrain or of mopping up the battlefield and seizing the arms booty. But they cannot prevent the NLF forces from launching large-scale ambushes and attacks and wiping out entire battalions or even regiments. This has been proven scores of times. American combat planes, helicopters and airborne artillery were incapable of saving the Americans and the mercenaries from serious defeats at Plei Me and other places. At Plei Me, despite the air power monopoly, the Americans abandoned dead and wounded on the battlefield. Even the monopoly of air power is not as all-powerful as it sounds.

"The NLF has no air force, but they have succeeded in destroying enemy planes in numbers that would be considered very creditable for any modern air force with first-class fighter pilots—over 900 in 1965 alone, most of them on the ground in strongly defended bases. The losses in planes and pilots in the South, if compared to their role in influencing the military situation, is costly out of all proportion to the damage done. Air power, in fact, has not paid anything like the dividends American military leaders expected. Some of them are now admitting this.

"Here, in the North, enemy planes have caused certain losses in men and material; they temporarily disturbed our transport system. But as we had foreseen, and as you have been able to confirm for yourself, air power cannot sabotage our largely agricultural economy, nor affect our regional industries, nor bring our transport and communications to a halt or even appreciably slow them down."

"What about helicopters?" I asked, and I reminded General Vinh that in 1962 he had said that the only technical innovation the Americans had introduced, as compared to the French, was the use of amphibious tanks and helicopters which had the advantage of surprise and mobility, new elements in guerrilla warfare.

"True," he replied, "they play an important role in increasing the mobility of enemy infantry; and a limited role in other missions, as firing platforms, for instance, or in transport of supplies and evacuation of wounded. But they also have their weaknesses in that they are slow-flying, virtually immobile at landing and take-off, easy to hit. While they can usually bring troops in when they want, they can't always take them out when they want, especially during the monsoon season when mist and clouds can suddenly blot out even the tree-tops. The fiasco of the helicoptered use of Saigon troops during the 'special warfare' phase was a rude reminder of the limitations of this type of warfare.

"Indeed, the massive reliance on helicopters is itself a confession of the enemy's weakness, his inability to open up and control communications or to occupy territory. There have been several occasions when American troops, after an action, fought among themselves not to be the last evacuated, as the defense perimeter around the landing field shrank and those left till last feared to be out-numbered and wiped out in a surprise attack. Even the American press has reported cases in which Americans fired on the mercenary troops struggling for their share of helicopter space on such occasions. If the Americans controlled roads and territory such shameless episodes would be avoided. But the troops know they have no chance of getting back to their bases if they have to move on foot. The helicopters do give great mobility to infantrymen, but reliance on helicopters has just the opposite effect—it pins troops down to within a few miles of the landing and take-off clearings. What has the much-vaunted First Airmobile Cavalry Division achieved in almost a year with its nearly 500 helicopters? It is still trying to secure an area a few miles around its An Khe base, where officers and men are still being picked off in the doorways of their billets by NLF snipers. Their helicopters cannot save them at such times when they are forced to engage in hand-to-hand fighting inside their own defense perimeter. Helicopters have certainly not turned out to be the miracle weapon the Americans counted on.

"There are other factors in our analyses which sometimes surprise our friends," General Vinh continued. "For example, despite the tremendous weight of material and technical power, which impresses so many western correspondents, we do not

consider the American military machine very efficient. The
French were better. We do not consider very competent either
the generals in the field, the Saigon command or the overall
direction from the Pentagon. We think they are especially weak
in their overall evaluations of specific situations—particularly
in relation to Vietnam."

"Despite the computers?" I asked. "They are supposed to be
infallible in their evaluations."

"Despite the computers," he replied, and he smiled and toyed
with a pencil for a while. "I suppose that computers can only
turn up the right answers if scientific, objective facts are supplied them. The CIA seems to have earned the reputation of
amassing data which is far from objective.

"In any case the military history of the USA testifies to the
fact that it is usually only at a moment favorable to them that
they decide on armed intervention. They have departed from
that rule here. In World War I, they waited until the Germans
were at the point of being beaten before they committed their
troops in 1917. In World War II, it was only after the decisive
victories of the Soviet Army had started the collapse of Hitler's
troops, that they opened the second front in Europe. In the
Pacific, it was the Japanese who forced their hand by attacking
Pearl Harbor. And there, they hastened to use the A-Bomb
for prestige reasons when they saw the Soviet Army and the
Chinese People's Liberation Army were on the point of wiping
out the formidable Kwantung Army in Manchuria and North
Korea. Later, in Korea and, more recently, in the Congo and
Dominican Republic, American troops were used either to halt
a situation critical for their imperialist interests or bring about
changes to their advantage.

"Computers or not, they were subjective in their evaluations
as to South Vietnam. Their whole strategic concept was wrong,
based on false premises. In Vietnam they thought that by sending a few hundreds of thousands of troops to the South and
intensifying their raids against the North they could bring about
decisive changes in their favor—specifically, to force the NLF
troops on the defensive, force them back into low-level guerrilla
activities and thus bring about capitulation in the South as in
the North. But here they violated their own rules. They inter-

vened when the situation was very unfavorable for them, when the Saigon army was demoralized and weak, when the army and administration, in fact, had started to disintegrate. The NLF forces, on the other hand, were strong, with the initiative everywhere in their hands, most of the country under their control, their morale high and a tide of revolutionary upsurge throughout the country. Thus, from the beginning the American forces have been mainly on the defensive. They have not been able to force the NLF to go back to guerrilla warfare; the Americans themselves complain that they have been subject to attacks at battalion and multi-battalion strength.

"The NLF troops have employed most varied tactics, almost invariably catching the Americans off balance. They have used direct assaults, ambushes, positional warfare, attacking posts and exterminating reinforcements, and commando attacks against US bases. They have displayed far greater mobility than the US troops, inflicting very heavy losses on the latter. True, the Americans try to compensate for their defeats by paper victories, victories by statistics. These may fool the American public for a while, but they don't fool American troops on the battlefield or their commanders, and far less the Pentagon. After a careful analysis of every important confrontation with American troops to date, we can conclude that the patriotic troops and population of South Vietnam are perfectly capable of defeating all categories of American troops under any circumstances."

General Vinh then went on to give thumbnail assessments of the various US units engaged in the ground war:

First Infantry Division: Though highly motorized and trained in conventional warfare, it is less mobile than the Saigon troops, once on the ground and operating in unfamiliar terrain. Hardly controlling any roads for the motorized equipment, morale is "deplorably low." In battles at Bau Bang and Nha Mat, within minutes of the first shots being fired, battalions of this division were sliced into sections by NLF assault teams and wiped out. Troops will not move without artillery bombardments and air strikes and in general will not start an operation unless they are convinced beforehand that they will not encounter their adversary. The NLF forces choose their own time and place in hitting this division, using the tactic of "grabbing the enemy by the belt" to deprive him of the advantage of air and artillery support.

18th Parachute Brigade: Its troops have hardly ever used their parachutes after the first venture at Thuan Ninh where they found they could only be successful "against an impressionable enemy whose rear is not secure." In the few cases they use their parachutes "they are received everywhere by a hostile terrain, by guerrillas and spiked fields, by regular troops who give them no chance to link up." Parachute operations, having scarcely been utilized in Vietnam, had already become an outmoded tactic. The parachutists hardly ever jump; they travel by helicopter or on foot, and are even less effective than other American specialized units.

First Airmobile Cavalry Division: The best equipped, most mobile division, conceived as the Pentagon's surest weapon in regaining the initiative in the High Plateaux, was beaten to the ground at the Plei Me-Ia Drang battle by foot-bound NLF troops. In their biggest action, the First Airmobile troops fled, abandoning their dead and wounded. It has proved its incapacity to operate in the forests and mountains of Central Vietnam where its super-mobility is neutralized by climate and nature; the morale of its troops is no better than in the Saigon army.

US Marines: Traditionally the Marines are used to effect landings and rapid assaults against islands and coastlines to open up the invasion route for the US army. But after their defeat at Van Tuong (which the Americans claim as their "victory at Chu Lai"), the Marines have been reduced to trying to protect their own bases as well as the Danang Air Base, and to patrol the area immediately surrounding these bases. In this they have acquitted themselves badly. Each of the bases they were assigned to defend has been repeatedly attacked from inside. In each of several defensive operations they have launched outside their bases they have been pushed back with heavy losses. NLF control of the countryside around the Danang and Chu Lai bases is more solid than when the Marines first landed. "A full Marine division and one Marine brigade, the most vaunted of all American fighting units, are in fact held in a pincer's grip by the NLF and their guerrillas," General Vinh continued. "Their heavy losses in the first big engagement at Van Tuong, was sufficient to end at one blow the main strategic concept with which the Americans began their invasion. This was the so-called 'ink blot' strategy by which the Marines would establish beachheads all along the coast, then expand outward like drops of ink on blotting paper, until they had occupied the whole coast. The regular army could then go on 'expanding' inland. 'Ink blot' was thrown overboard after the Van Tuong action. The whole coastline still remains a theater of operations for guerrillas.

"Since the Americans themselves write so much about their logistics problems in supplying their 230,000-odd troops now in South Vietnam, it is not necessary for me to go into details about that," General Vinh said. "But we can say with certainty that the military bases and logistics system will never be guaranteed security from the daring and expert blows of the NLF and local guerrillas. The capital defect of these bases is that they can never be properly defended and this will become ever more apparent as supply problems grow with increased troops. It is impossible to overestimate all the difficulties; the interruptions of the American transport and logistics system will increase in the future. When the Americans claim that they are capable of fighting on for decades with a battle corps of 500,000, 700,000 or 1,000,000 troops, this is not a well-founded or well-meditated opinion. Because of all the factors I have enumerated," he said in conclusion, "we believe in the inevitable defeat of the enemy and our own victory. And don't forget that we have always considered that victory will come as a combination of military-political activity, which from the start has been the very essence of our resistance strategy."

Only time will tell whether General Vinh's computation was well-founded. What is certain is that it took into account many elements such as tradition, nature, climate, psychology, morale and social and political factors, difficult to conceive as being available, or acceptable, to the Pentagon computers.

Chapter 11

HANOI—CAPITAL WITH A QUESTION MARK

As one walks the quiet streets of Hanoi it is difficult to imagine that 10,000 miles away it is being decided whether to wipe it out or not. Children play with wooden guns around the air-raid shelters. The few young couples still left stroll arm-in-arm or sit head-to-head on the seats around the Petit Lac in the center of the city; the stream of cycle-borne traffic at midday, the flower-stalls spilling out on to the footpaths. It would doubtless be fascinating to snatch a glimpse at the "pro" and "con" data being fed into the computers, and at the thought processes of President Johnson as he ponders over whatever advice the computers pass on.

Hanoi is not a glamorous or exotic city. To many visitors from the West, socialist countries included, it is a drab, grey city. It is in fact a poor city; at best the government has succeeded in stabilizing poverty and avoiding misery. The changes for the better that mark the countryside have left little impact on the capital, superficially at least. No efforts have been made to make it a prestige showplace as is customary for a capital city. Perhaps this was a mistake. More effort should have been made, a bigger investment in paint and repairs at least. It is a mistake hardly likely to be corrected now. The few luxury shops that existed to serve a privileged section of the population in the past disappeared with the privileges. This was to be expected. The privileged in the old days were the foreigners, top government officials and rich merchants.

Government officials are, if anything, the under-privileged these days, the President and Prime Minister themselves setting the example in austerity and frugality by living in the former servants' quarters of the former French governor-general's palace. This is not demagogy. It is a continuation of their life, and that of the thousands of other devoted cadres, of the first resistance. It accords with the economic situation of the country. When President Ho Chi Minh was about to read the Declaration of Independence, on September 2, 1945, it was realized at the last moment that he had no suitable clothes. He had come from the jungle with old khaki shorts and a pair of automobile-tire sandals and little else. A hasty shopping expedition produced a khaki suit and a pair of manufactured rubber sandals, Ho Chi Minh's concession to protocol.

The rich merchants and the privileged officials and many who lived off them left in any case for Saigon, when the separation of combatants took place after the 1954 Geneva Agreements. The foreign community also left. Another foreign community arrived from the socialist world with neither the tastes nor ready cash to form a clientele for the bars and restaurants and luxury shops—or to finance by their patronage the neon signs, or even the paint, to maintain the color and glamor common to most Asian capitals. The Government certainly had neither foreign exchange nor any interest in importing the sort of goods stocked in the former luxury shops, even if customers could be found. Hence, useless to pretend otherwise, Hanoi has presented a drab, austere face to the outside world these recent years and it has grown drabber and more austere as the war clouds gathered over the border in Laos and south of the 17th parallel.

To even slightly raise the living standards of the peasants meant cutting into the standards of the urban middle class. Economic policy aimed, if not at egalitarianism, at least at greatly reducing the differences between salaries and wages and between urban and rural living standards. The few automobiles on the streets were used by top-ranking government officials, usually ministers and vice-ministers, on very strictly official business, or by visiting delegations and the diplomatic corps. Traffic is sufficiently sparse to insure that every automobile has individual attention from the police at street intersections. There has been virtually no rebuilding inside the city at all in 12 years of socialist power. Goods on display are sadly lacking in variety and quality, apart from a few shops selling traditional art and handicraft work, lacquer paintings, ivory carvings, silverwork and a variety of woven baskets, table mats and other items mainly bought by foreigners.

These are the aspects that first impress visitors from the West, especially those who knew Hanoi before, when it was the bustling capital of French power in Indochina with brightly lit streets, bars in every block, shops full of French consumer goods, the streets jammed with limousines, not to mention officers' staff cars and military traffic in general. For Vietnamese, however, the picture seems different. The goods in the state shops correspond to their needs and their pocket books, and besides they are now all made in the country. Thermos flasks, bicycles, textiles, flash lamps, electric light bulbs, enamel ware, cigarettes and matches, soap, all sorts of household tools and modest kitchen gadgets, plastic raincoats and footwear, the daily necessities of life are there and at reasonable prices—ridiculously cheap if priced at official exchange rates, but reasonable also in terms of people's low earnings.

The improvements that had been made in people's lives were not all visible, like shorter working hours, paid holidays and pensions and other benefits not expressed in shop windows and neon lights.

Although there are almost no new buildings in the city itself, when one drives into the outskirts the picture is more impressive. In one direction, are many newly built factories, turning out the electric light bulbs, thermos flasks, cigarettes and the other consumer goods to be found in the shops; in another direction, bigger plants turning out machine tools, electric generators and transformers, diesel maritime engines and motors for pumping stations. If one takes still another turn there are the new institutes for Economics and Finance, Medicine and Pharmacy, Economic Planning, National Minorities, Agricultural Science, Theater and Cinema, and others—most of them modest, two- or three-story buildings. Well spaced, often surrounded by rice fields, they stretch for many miles from the capital. These were impressive by any standards, not so much the buildings but what they represented in investment for the future. They help to balance the drab, provincial aspect of the capital.

Oddly enough it is the occasional visitor from Saigon who is the least critical of Hanoi. The contrast between the calm and normality of life there with the feverish war-torn atmosphere of Saigon, even before the great American invasion, seems like balm to the Saigon visitor. No traffic noise, no screaming sirens of police and military cars, no tanks churning through the streets, no security patrols, no lurid sex and crime movie ads. No payment expected for smiles in hotels and restaurants. No touts, pimps, beggars, prostitutes, no inflation. And even for hardened topers the very absence of a half dozen bars in every block was more of a relief than a hardship. Many a foreigner stationed in Hanoi begins to take a fresh look at the city after his first ten minutes with a visitor from Saigon. (Because of the International Control Commission's commutation between both capitals, such visitors were not so rare).

Within its austere, frugal framework, Hanoi in fact has its charm and the Hanoi-dwellers have their quiet, modest pleasures. The Petit Lac in the very center of the city is a gem, bordered by huge, shady trees and with an ancient pagoda rising up out of the water, linked to the shore with a stone bridge. Around the lake, small stalls sell drinks ranging from fresh coconut milk through various soft drinks to Hanoi beer (very good and very cheap). Disputing the space with the refreshment kiosks these days are the air-raid shelters which completely surround the lake. The central parts of many of the wider streets are also taken up with air-raid shelters, and the footpaths of narrow streets are lined with individual cylindrical shelters with covers, the latter being removed by air-raid wardens or "clients" as soon as an alert sounds. Most of the communal shelters are covered with earth on which flowers and sometimes vegetables flourish. In a street near the hotel where I stayed one big shelter was sprouting maize.

One end of the Petit Lac leads into the European part of the city, built by the French, with plenty of broad leafy avenues and solid double-story villas, the best of them now occupied by diplomats. The other end of the lake leads into the ancient Vietnamese section of the city. Here the streets are laid out as in European Middle Age cities, on a craft basis. Thirty-six such streets remain, many of the crafts represented by the old names only. Silk street was the best known to foreigners, but there are also streets of the gold and silversmiths, of workers in jade and ivory, brass workers, tinsmiths, leather workers, wooden-chest and coffin-makers and so on. In some of them, the crafts are still pursued, in others the craftsmen were formed into cooperatives and in certain cases they moved into industry. What with inroads in industry, lack of clients for luxury goods—and now the evacuation of non-essential personnel—the craft streets have also lost their bustle and fascination.

There is White Bamboo lake, a bustling place on a Saturday and Sunday with its little dinghies gliding over the water and a much-patronized open-air restaurant, specializing in shrimp fritters (the shrimp passing literally from lake to frying pan) washed down with beer, which has become a national beverage over the past few years. One of the attractions of Hanoi is its many lakes, including the big Unity lake recently built by VPA men and members of the Labor Youth Union in their spare time, complete with well-kept flower beds and enough stone seats around the shore to accommodate a high proportion of the city's young couples. But, compared to previous visits, they seemed mainly occupied by old people now.

Ba Dinh square, in the heart of the European quarter and within a stone's throw of the former French governor-general's palace, is today to Hanoi what the Red Square is to Moscow or the Tien An Men to Peking. It was here that Ho Chi Minh read the Declaration of Independence, written, as he said, "with the blood and tears of patriots, shed during more than 80 years." The Declaration was based on an eight-point document that Ho Chi Minh had submitted to Woodrow Wilson, Clemenceau, Lloyd George and other world leaders at the Versailles Peace Conference in 1919, when Nguyen Ai Quoc, as President Ho Chi Minh was then known, raised for the first time the question of Vietnamese independence. It incorporated passages from the American Declaration of Independence and the French Declaration of the Rights of Man and Citizen.

It is worth recalling today that within four months of independence having been proclaimed, general elections were held throughout all of Vietnam—there was no demarcation line along the 17th parallel in those days. Ambassador Cabot Lodge in an interview with the Columbia Broadcasting System in Saigon on April 22, 1966, explaining his extreme suspicion of elections in Vietnam, even those promised by Premier Nguyen Cao Ky, said that they were an "untrod path." He then made the singularly uninformed remark that the Vietnamese people "have never before had elections on a national basis and a national question. It's never happened in their whole history."

The nationwide elections which took place on January 6, 1946, gave the Vietminh candidates 230 seats in the National Assembly. On March 3, 1946, Ho Chi Minh was elected president of the Republic and three days later France, through its representative in Hanoi, M. Jean Sainteny, recognized the DRV as "a free state having its own government, parliament and finance." On September 14 of the same year a *modus vivendi* was signed between the governments of the DRV and France, at Fontainebleau, confirming the March 6th agreement. One of the most respected American academic specialists on Vietnam, Ellen J. Hammer, wrote of the 1946 elections that even "had the elections been conducted to the strictest of Western forms, a few more conservatives might have been chosen" but the outcome would have been the same (*The Struggle for Indochina*, Stanford Un. Press, 1954). Strange that Ambassador Cabot Lodge should be so ill-informed, especially as it was precisely the fear that the results of the 1946 elections would have been confirmed, perhaps even more decisively, in 1956 that prompted Washington to avoid at any cost the elections which, according to the Geneva Agreements, should have taken place in July that year. In the eyes of most observers, the decision not to hold those elections is the single, most fundamental reason for the present conflict.

Ba Dinh square these days is adorned with a modest, wooden tribune where leaders and distinguished guests greet the Hanoi population on Independence Day and on other occasions for celebration. It is one of the capital's showplaces for history-minded visitors.

For visitors with an interest in more ancient times there is a fascinating exhibit in Hanoi's history museum which provides a direct link between military tactics of the Vietnamese today and those of their ancestors. When Ngo Quyen destroyed the fleet of the Southern Han invaders in 938 A.D. and Tran Hung Dao destroyed the 400-odd warships of the Mongols invaders in 1288, they employed tactics and techniques adopted since by the NLF forces in the South against helicopters, parachutists and other marauders, and by certain anti-aircraft gunners against US planes in the North.

The history museum displays remnants of stout pointed stakes, six to nine feet long that were driven deep into the bed of the Bach Dang river, north of present-day Haiphong, the traditional invasion route for Vietnam's enemies in those days. In the place from which the museum pieces were taken—a number of such instances are recorded in Vietnamese history—200 such stakes were embedded over an area 130 yards long by 22 yards wide. The tactic was for the shallow-draught Vietnamese warships to pretend to flee upstream, luring the enemy fleet after them at high tide when the stakes were well covered by the river. When the tide turned and the river raced to the sea, the enemy ships were also forced to race seaward or be grounded on the river bed. The lighter Vietnamese warships then started in hot pursuit, catching up with the Chinese and Mongol fleets, in their respective centuries, as they were wedged in among the stout stakes, the fast-receding waters leaving them high and dry either to capsize or present themselves as easy targets for the Vietnamese fire-arrows. In between the Southern Hans and the Mongols, another Chinese fleet (the Songs) was similarly trapped in 981 A.D.

Helicopter pilots have found to their cost that many of the only landing fields around Vietcong-chosen battlefields are similarly studded with sharp, six-foot high stakes that foul propellers or pierce the fuselage. And parachutists have given up jumping since they found that harmless-looking elephant grass and other foliage that covered ideal jumping areas, in fact, concealed extensive nests of needle-sharp spikes. In the North, ingenious devices have been used to lure American planes to fake targets, most advantageous for the anti-aircraft gunners, and occasionally MIG pilots, to get them in their sights.

One thing which astonishes the visitor from the West is that the pith helmet (*casque coloniale*), without which no caricature of an imperialist is complete in the former colonies of Asia and Africa, is almost standard headgear in North Vietnam. From President Ho Chi Minh down, soldiers and civilians of both sexes, wear the pith helmet, now produced locally from a sort of synthetic cork. Its advantages of lightness and protection against the sun have won out over prejudices arising from its colonialist origin. Those worn by soldiers today are flecked with bits of green cloth camouflage.

If there are only few cars in the streets, there are plenty of truck convoys in the outskirts, each truck with a plywood projection of its roof to prevent reflections from the windshield attracting the attention of planes, and roofs and sides heavily draped in greenery. Buses which link Hanoi with the provincial capitals are also heavily camouflaged, their windows blackened and decorated with strips and sheets of paper to prevent the glass splintering from bomb blast. Windows of schools and hospitals still functioning in Hanoi are similarly "decorated"— and the word is not out of place because, with the humor and natural artistic sense of the Vietnamese people, the paper is cut in attractive patterns like the Chinese paper-cuts stuck on to windows and screens in the villages in China, authentic forms of folk art. Ironically enough, the windows of one wing of Hanoi's TB hospital were decorated with Picasso "peace doves," some others with heroes and heroines of Vietnamese opera, mixed with an infinite variety of pure geometric patterns.

Strolling on the streets of Hanoi, mingling with the invariably good-humored crowd, pairs of Bo Doi (soldiers) strolling hand in hand, the trams rattling along with baskets of chickens and vegetables hanging out of the windows, crowds pouring out of cinemas (which have become immensely popular since non-evacuated husbands and other family members have more free time on their hands) to gather at a street corner while the tally of downed planes is adjusted on the local scoreboard, an outsider is hardly conscious of what is in everyone's minds—when will the bombs start falling?

There is no atmosphere of nervousness, but everyone has some family members evacuated or is preparing his own evacuation. Conversation in factories and offices every Monday morning turns on exchanges of experience of those who have been able to visit their children in the villages the previous day. The lives of every family in Hanoi have been turned upside down because of the expectation of bombardment. The noise level of modern jets and the explosive force of the bombs are such that almost daily raids 20 or 25 miles outside the capital are clearly audible.

Hanoi residents hear their fate being discussed over the radio. There is no disapproval of listening to the Voice of America or Radio Saigon—"You can compare their lies with our reality," is the official view. They listen to the differing views of "hawks" and "doves" as to whether their capital should be wiped out or not.

When one ponders over this and tries to visualize just what would happen, it can be considered a blessing for Hanoi residents that their lives were not dramatically changed, in a material sense, in the years of peace. It may even prove fortunate that the government did not rush to build multi-story ministries or blocks of offices and apartments, although this could have been justified for a million-population capital of a newly independent state. From a practical point of view, there are no lifts or subways for people to be trapped in because of power failures in a bombing raid; no thousands of deep-freezers each with scores of dollars' worth of food inside to spoil; no lines of automobiles to jam up because traffic lights cease to function— nothing to cause the panic and fantastic breakdown that occured in New York and other American East Coast cities in the power failures of autumn 1965. Nor are there any skyscraper buildings to come tumbling down in the event of bombs, to trap hundreds of people in their ruins and block off entire streets with their debris. If "the worst comes" those left in Hanoi can be in their flower-topped shelters within seconds.

I have seen Hanoi in varying moods, but for very special reasons the most vivid impressions were the first—because the "first" in this case was the entry of the VPA into Hanoi after the 1954 Geneva Agreements were signed.

Looking back over what I wrote then, I find that in a certain sense it expresses the mood today, as hundreds of thousands of young people take off from Hanoi to complete the work of their fathers and older brothers.

The transfer of power in Hanoi in October 1954 was a block-by-block, street-by-street process, the lightly equipped VPA troops marching in on their famous "Ho Chi Minh" tire sandals, as the motorized convoys of French troops moved out. Backed up behind the VPA troops were Hanoi residents, flags and banners in hand:

"Along the footpaths, the people moved exactly level with the foremost VPA soldier, stopping when he stopped, moving as he advanced, the flood swelling in volume as the transfer penetrated deeper and deeper into the city. Discipline of the population was as perfect as that of the troops. Appeals had been made by the VPA Command for calm and order, to avoid any pretexts for provocations. And so it was. Everything was calm and orderly, but as the VPA took over street by street, block by block, the city blossomed into life. Flags from doors and windows kept pace with the advance, banners right across the streets a few minutes later and within the next few hours, solid welcoming arches covered with peace doves, portraits of President Ho, slogans, banners, lanterns, everything that symbolized peace, victory, jubilation. . . ."

The following day, the ceremonial entry of the VPA took place.

"The whole of the population turned out next day in their best clothes; city women in gossamer-light, pastel-colored silk tunics and trousers; peasant women in their chocolate-colored blouse and broad, black trousers; elderly men in their dignified long black, silk tunics, white silk trousers and stiff round caps; younger men mostly in European-style white shirts and slacks, everyone waving flags and flowers, hurling bouquets into passing trucks, children with flowers rushing out to embrace and be embraced by the cheerful troops, the moment there was a halt in the convoy.

"American trucks, American jeeps, American artillery, American bazookas, machine guns, and anti-aircraft guns passed through the wildly cheering lines of people. . . .

"The excitement was intensified when word passed round, from relatives who recognized them, that the troops taking part in the ceremonial entry were from Hanoi's own regiment, formed from Hanoi's young workers, intellectuals, students and other patriots, who fought the French behind barricades in Hanoi in a most heroic episode at the very beginning of the resistance war. They had left almost eight years previously in rags and tatters, armed with a few aged rifles, carrying their wounded with them after two months of barricade and house-to-house fighting. When further resistance was impossible, they capped their extraordinary feat by slipping out at night, under the very noses of the French and crossed the Red River, *underneath* the two kilometre-long Paul Doumer bridge which joins Hanoi with the suburb of Gia Lam. They moved back to the hinterland to prepare for the long fight ahead.

"Mothers, fathers and wives in the welcoming crowd had difficulty in recognizing their sons and husbands in these noble veterans, spick and span in their VPA uniforms, sitting in neat rows in powerful trucks bearing designations showing they had fought at Dien Bien Phu, manning artillery pieces and complicated anti-aircraft guns, others marching with disciplined swinging steps, battle-hardened veterans, but not hardened enough to prevent tears from rolling down their cheeks at the sight of a beloved face not seen for eight years, the voice of a mother, father, wife or child in a gasping shout of recognition as the trucks and columns of marching men swept on.

"The tattered heroes of the barricade battle were the nucleus around which was later built the Hanoi regiment, now part of the elite 308th Division. Theirs was the first big battle fought by the young resistance army. The resistance dates, in fact, from the moment Hanoi's young workers, students and patriots took to the barricades that night, and fought their epic two months' battle gaining precious time for resistance to be organized in the hinterland, for roads and bridges to be destroyed to hold up French plans to push ahead and wipe out the resistance bases in the Viet Bac (the northern provinces). They were designated a battalion during their barricade battle and later, reinforced by a steady flow of recruits fleeing the city, were formed into a regiment, one that took part in every important battle up to and including Dien Bien Phu. Now the Hanoi Regiment had come back home and the once powerful adversary was pulling out ahead of them, dragging away the guns and technique which had been defeated by the superior morale of a people fighting in a just cause. . . .

"For many, it was on and past Hanoi to other districts, other tasks. Every soldier and every cadre knew there would be no real relaxation until the whole of Vietnam was liberated and united. For many, it was a question of a quick embrace, a hugging of wife or child in the arms, a few whispered words,

tears struggling with smiles, smiles with tears and on to the new
tasks. And the miracle was that this was something willingly
accepted in a proud, disciplined way. No one who witnessed
these momentary reunions could doubt the depth of their emo-
tions, their love of family, their yearning for permanent reunion.
One could only marvel at their discipline, their understanding
and acceptance of the need for further sacrifices, so that all
could enjoy tomorrow what they must renounce today." (From
North of the 17th Parallel, 1955.)

How many of them have again said goodbye to wives and
children and sweethearts to press on with, what seems for them,
the same old task with the same sense of discipline and self-
sacrifice? Not only do those who leave seem to accept it as
normal. But also those who stay. I have lots of friends in Hanoi,
but I never heard a single grumble, except against the Americans and against those who suggest they should compromise
with the enemy.

Will similar scenes be repeated in Saigon? A similar ceremonial entry of the NLF and a block-by-block, street-by-street
withdrawal of American forces? Generals Giap and Vinh in the
North, and Nguyen Huu Tho, president of the NLF in the
South, are counting on it. If so what will be left of Hanoi by
that time? That is a big question mark.

In this connection, I have heard some original ideas expressed
in high places in Hanoi, amongst other, the following: "If it is
destroyed, so what? We'll build it again, better than it ever
was. We'll build a modern, Vietnamese city. As it is, Hanoi is
half foreign, half feudal. We don't agree with what the Czechs
did. They opened their frontiers to foreign invaders without a
fight because Hitler threatened to bomb Prague. They paid for
that with over five years of Nazi occupation. The French gave
up half their country to the Nazis and the other half to their
own fascists to save Paris. We will never do this. That's a bour-
geois concept of fighting a war. We will never cede anything
to save the capital."

Even when it is pointed out that Paris and Prague were not
foreign but very much French and Czech creations, and not
feudal cities but the product of centuries of growth during

various stages of society, it was still argued that "no country or principle should ever be sacrificed for a city."

An interesting item to feed into the Pentagon computers when they ruminate over the fate of Hanoi, would be a reminder that the Vietminh fought their first resistance war without having Hanoi, Haiphong or any other major city in their hands and with virtually all provincial capitals and strategic roads in the hands of their adversary. Also: although the two months' rear-guard battle fought by Hanoi's workers in 1945 facilitated the removal of a certain amount of equipment from the capital to the jungle, this was infinitesimal compared to the complete industrial units removed this time and already producing in safe hide-outs. But the key question that should be fed in is: "After destroying Hanoi and Haiphong—what next?" That would really embarrass the computers, since even Defense Secretary McNamara is said to have misgivings now as to whether it would make an iota of difference to his problems in South Vietnam. In having psychologically prepared the Hanoi and Haiphong residents that their cities would almost certainly be bombed, the Vietnamese leaders in fact neutralized what McNamara certainly considered his "ace" weapon in the escalation arsenal.

Chapter 12

THE DIFFICULT PEACE

Trying to see how this will all end seems like trying to find the answer to the old conundrum of what happens when an irresistible force meets an immovable object. The short answer in human affairs is that the break comes when one side becomes convinced that it is no longer an "irresistible force" or the other recognizes that it is not in fact an "immovable object." So far neither Hanoi nor Washington have realistically set out the precise steps that could be taken to end the war. It is much simpler in fact to foresee how the war will continue than how it will end. By May 1966, what with the stalemate on the military front in the South and the revolt in Danang and Hue, the backroom experts at General Westmoreland's headquarters in Saigon were privately briefing correspondents along these lines: "Granted, we cannot win the war in the South in the *South*. But we will win the war in the South in the North—by breaking the North." About the time this new thesis was launched, the tempo of air raids against the North was stepped up by the use of B-52's and a series of attacks on urban centers.

This was the subject of the first question I put to Prime Minister Pham Van Dong in an interview on the lawns of the former French governor-general's palace.

"The Americans think and now say that they can win the war in South Vietnam by crushing North Vietnam. What do you think about that?"

"It's an unspeakable crime," replied Pham Van Dong, "and at the same time a gross mistake, the consequences of which will fall on their own heads.

"They are bogged down in the South and they are suffering heavy losses in the North of our country. It appears that they are planning to extend the war to other countries of Indochina, to Laos for a start. Well, they are creating the conditions for their own defeat and on a scale that they cannot imagine."

Pham Van Dong has filled out and mellowed a good deal

from the days, 12 years previously when he made his debut at the 1954 Geneva Conference for the cease-fire negotiations, with the bonus of the Dien Bien Phu victory in his pocket. His eyes have lost that burning look which many who met him for the first time in those days attributed to his revolutionary ardor, but which in fact was a consequence of chronic malaria acquired during six years in the cells of the island prison at Poulo Condor. A few grey hairs at the temples—he is now 60—a bronzed, very human, kindly face, he radiated good health, good humor and an exuberant confidence. An enthusiastic soccer player in his youth, he is still keen on physical exercise and during a break in the interview he earnestly advised me to follow his example and do 15 minutes of calisthenics every morning.

Like Vo Nguyen Giap, with whom he was intimately associated in the early days of the Vietnamese revolution, Pham Van Dong was a geography and history teacher in a French school in Saigon. In the mid-1920's, while Ho Chi Minh (Nguyen Ai Quoc, or Nguyen the Patriot in those days) was in Canton, training future cadres and knitting the various threads of revolutionary struggle together, Pham Van Dong also went there for training. He returned to carry on similar work inside the country, above all secretly organizing an underground trade union movement, and later, strikes of mine and rubber plantation workers. Arrested in 1929, he was sentenced to 10 years at Poulo Condor, the equivalent of a death sentence because of the terrible conditions there, but was released when the Popular Front government came to power in France in 1936.

Four years later he left again for China, this time with Vo Nguyen Giap, to join the headquarters set up by Ho Chi Minh. Back in North Vietnam, after the Vietminh was formed on May 19, 1941 (Ho Chi Minh's 51st birthday), he and Giap continued the brick-by-brick construction of political bases in the North. By the end of 1944 things had advanced sufficiently to launch the armed struggle. A first platoon, named after Tran Hung Dao (of river-stakes fame against the Mongols), was set up with Vo Nguyen Giap in charge. Its 34 members were armed with 17 bolt-rifles, 14 flintlocks and two revolvers. The date of the formation of the Tran Hung Dao platoon, December 22,

1944, is now celebrated as the foundation date of the VPA. At this time Ho Chi Minh was shuffling up and down the mountains of Kwangsi province arms tied behind his back, his feet in chains, being transferred from one Kuomintang prison to another.

Very typical for the energetic Giap was the fact that a few hours after the platoon was formed it launched a night attack, wiping out two enemy posts and capturing a precious stock of weapons to replace its flintlocks and arm the nucleus of further platoons. By the time Ho Chi Minh was released from jail and returned to Vietnam, six provinces in the Viet Bac or north of the country had been liberated and had their own administration, set up by Pham Van Dong. Giap was pushing further south, but a solid revolutionary base had been secured. Pham Van Dong was one of the members of the National Liberation Committee set up in August 1945, on the eve of the general insurrection in which state power was seized from the Japanese. He became Minister of Finance in the first government. When French forces attacked Hanoi at the end of 1946, the government moved back into the Viet Bac bases set up by Pham Van Dong in 1944. He, together with Vo Nguyen Giap, remained at Ho Chi Minh's side during the eight hard years of struggle which led to Dien Bien Phu and the 1954 Geneva Conference.

Now, here he was, seated at a table on the lawns of the former French governor-general's palace which is now the President's Residence (the servants' quarters of which Pham Van Dong now shares with Ho Chi Minh), replying to my questions about a very different type of war.

"The government of the DRV repeatedly has stated that it is prepared to wage a long war, for ten, 15 or more years," I said. "Have you taken steps for such a long war?"

"A national liberation war is by its nature, a people's war, a long war, one that can last for tens of years. Our people are fighting for their liberty, their life, their honor. They fight for real peace based on real independence. They will fight on till victory, no matter what the cost.

"The logic of this war is the following: For the Americans, each time the Pentagon 'hawks' move on to some new phase of 'escalation,' they do so only because of previous setbacks which have brought them to the verge of total collapse. This means that for us, in the South as in the North, the perspectives are not only for further very important victories but also for an accelerated build-up of our people's forces in every field, above all in the armed forces. Under such conditions the higher the 'hawks' fly the heavier they will fall."

"Does not all this necessarily imply a setback for your plans for building socialism?" I asked.

"Absolutely the contrary. Not only do we continue to build socialism, but we are stepping up the tempo in many fields in order to satisfy our wartime needs.

"We are living through an extraordinary epoch in our history. We are witnessing a veritable flowering of the traditional virtues of our people—courage, energy, intelligence, love for the Motherland, faith in victory. It is this that explains our victories in the struggle against American aggression and our progress in developing agriculture, regional industry and in the fields of culture, science and technique."

"What are the present possibilities of ending the war? Is there no possibility of negotiations until the bombings of the North have definitively stopped? And is it only with the NLF of South Vietnam that the Americans must negotiate an end to the war in the South?" I asked.

"Our position on this subject," replied Pham Van Dong, "has been most clearly set out by President Ho Chi Minh, in his letter of last January 21 to the heads of state of a number of countries.

"First, our four-point proposal.

"Second, definite and unconditional halt to bombings and all other acts of war against the DRV.

"Third, as for the problems of South Vietnam, it is necessary to talk with the National Liberation Front of South Vietnam, the only authentic representative of our compatriots in the South.

"You see that our position is simple, precise and clear. It is a position for peace, real peace based on our national independence."

"How do you evaluate the recent events in Saigon, Danang, Hue and other South Vietnam cities?" (At the time of the interview, the revolt occasioned by the dismissal of General Thi by Saigon was occurring in Central Vietnam.)

"What is inevitable is bound to happen," replied the Prime Minister, shrugging his shoulders and spreading his hands. "It is the reply of our people in the towns to the American expeditionary corps and their puppets. It is the inevitable result of the patriotic struggle and the people's war which is bringing off resounding victories all over the place.

"All this is part of an irreversible process. It will continue to develop in force, with incomparable richness of form until final victory."

President Ho Chi Minh came along just as the interview was finishing, clad, like Pham Van Dong, in a simple, khaki uniform, rosy of cheek, hale, hearty and full of smiles. It was just a couple of weeks short of his 76th birthday. He agreed to reply to just one question, but in English as well as in French. I asked him what he thought about the thesis of "breaking the North to win in the South."

President Ho laughed for a while before replying. "The Americans are deceiving themselves," he said, "in thinking that by bombing the North they can win in the South. Never, never will they win this war. Never, never will we submit—because this is a patriotic war, a just war, and we are determined to fight on if it takes five, ten, 20 or even more years. We will win this war because we are in the right, because we are supported by almost everybody, including Americans."

If the phrase "five, ten, 20 or more years" had come from anyone other than Pham Van Dong and Ho Chi Minh, it would have sounded by this time like stock propaganda; I had already heard it so often. But as the phrase had been initiated by President Ho himself and as he had started what seemed an even more impossible struggle, not five or 20 years but over 40 years ago, then it should be taken very seriously indeed. In his mouth it was not a slogan but the program of action which was being put into execution everywhere. Almost half a century ago, Ho Chi Minh had started to think in organizational terms of what was still only a dream in the minds of even the most advanced of his compatriots. Son of a mandarin scholar who had voluntarily renounced his office to become a peasant again because he loathed serving a foreign invader, Ho Chi Minh had about the roughest apprenticeship in revolution that is possible to imagine. But it nurtured in him a broad world culture and profound international outlook. There is no leader, in the western world, the communist world or the "third" world who has had comparable experiences.

In early 1912, having completed a three-months' training course in Saigon, a certain "Ba" signed aboard the French windjammer *Latouche Treville* as cook's helper. The name which his father had given him at the age of ten, in accordance with local tradition, had been Nguyen Tat Thanh, "Nguyen the Victorious," but his father, the mandarin-peasant, had no idea that the first step toward the brilliant fulfillment of this name was being taken in such unpromising circumstances. When he started slicing up his first bucket of potatoes, "Ba" had one burning thought in his mind, national independence, but no idea how to transform thought into reality.

But when his ship docked at Marseilles "Ba" made an important discovery which he never forgot. After his first visits to the cafes, he reported back to his shipmates: "The French in France are better and more polite than those in Indochina." Later, after a voyage to Africa in which he learned about four Senegalese at Dakar who drowned one after another trying to get a shore-line aboard a French ship, he said: "In France, the French are good. But the French colonialists are cruel and inhuman. . . . To them the life of an Asian or African is not worth a cent." From his first contacts with France, the future president Ho made a clear difference between French colonial power which he had sworn to overthrow and the French people whom he admired and respected.

In London in 1913 he worked for a time under the great French chef Escoffier at the Carlton Hotel; but in his spare time he studied the history of French and British colonialism and learned English, which he speaks today with a French accent that most English visitors to Hanoi find quite charming.

In France at the end of World War I, he changed his name again to Nguyen Ai Quoc (Nguyen the Patriot) and, at first as a photographer's retoucher then as a journalist, he organized the Vietnamese Association in whose name he presented an eight-point claim to Vietnamese independence to the allied powers at the Versailles Peace Conference. Later he formed a wider organization, the League of Colonial Countries, which embraced revolutionary groups from several of France's African and Asian colonies. He published and edited the League's underground paper *Le Paria* (The Pariah).

In 1924 he went to Moscow hoping to see Lenin and interest him in the struggle he intended launching in Vietnam, but Lenin had died two days before he arrived. In Moscow he studied revolutionary and organizational methods, adding the Russian language to his linguistic repertory. The following year he went to China, living first as a cigarette and newspaper vendor, but later working in Canton as secretary-translator to Borodin, who headed the Comintern Advisory Mission to Sun Yat-sen, founder of the first Chinese Republic. It was the honeymoon period of Kuomintang-Communist cooperation. A revolutionary government had been set up in Canton, Chou En-lai was political head of the Whampoa Military Academy which was turning out cadres to consolidate revolutionary power throughout China. In charge of the Academy was Chiang Kai-shek, he and Chou En-lai having in fact equal status.

Nguyen Ai Quoc was delighted with this situation and for the first time began to visualize how a movement could be organized in Vietnam. The success of the revolution in China would open the way for victory in Vietnam, he felt. Canton then was in a ferment and attracted revolutionaries from all over Asia. Nguyen threw himself into the movement with all his energies and talent. Typical of his international outlook, now in Canton he organized Koreans, Indonesians, Vietnamese and others into a League of Oppressed Peoples of Asia, just as previously in Paris he had formed the League of Colonial Countries. He also set up the League of Revolutionary Vietnamese Youth which was to become the chief source of cadres for the future liberation struggle. Among those who came to Canton at that time (1925), for training in revolutionary techniques was a young student in trouble with the authorities for having taken a leading part in a students' strike at the French *College du Protectorat* in Hanoi; this was Pham Van Dong. With Chinese help, under the newly adopted name of Vuong and never revealing to any but his most intimate collaborators that he was the already legendary Nguyen Ai Quoc, he was by this time publishing and smuggling into Vietnam newspapers and other publications which attracted almost equal interest among the French police and Vietnamese intellectuals.

In 1927, when Chiang Kai-shek broke with the Communists, slaughtering them by the thousands in Canton and Shanghai, Borodin and other Comintern advisers narrowly escaping with their lives to return to the Soviet Union, Nguyen moved into Thailand. Here he set up the Vietnamese Association for Mutual Assistance and a weekly organ *l'Humanité*, which was soon finding its way into Vietnam. There he added "Father Chin" to his list of names and Thai to his language stock, needless to say, having perfected his Chinese while in Canton. As the result of Nguyen's initiative three separate revolutionary groups had been set up in Vietnam. In late 1929, delegates from these three groups came out to a secret meeting with Nguyen Ai Quoc at Kweilin, in the Chinese province of Kwangsi which borders on Vietnam. The outcome was the formation of the Communist Party of Indochina on February 3, 1930.

Nguyen continued to work from outside while the cells he had implanted inside Vietnam continued to thrive and multiply, despite the setbacks—a major one occurred in 1929 when Pham Van Dong after his return from Canton had been discovered and arrested. Always on the move, always living frugally, always under a different name when his compatriots met him, feigning ignorance of the whereabouts or fate of Nguyen Ai Quoc, he saw to it that the familiar, clear, trenchant articles signed under this name appeared regularly in the illegal publications. With the French, Kuomintang or British police constantly on his trail, Nguyen Ai Quoc was reported several times to have died in one or another of their prisons. Jailed once in Hong Kong, he was released, took a ship to Singapore, was hauled off it and returned to the jails of Hong Kong again. Eventually released by the good offices of a British lawyer, he was spirited away to China, then to the Soviet Union. By the time World War II broke out, Nguyen Ai Quoc was back on the frontiers of Vietnam again. When the French in Indochina capitulated to the Japanese there was a meeting between

Nguyen Ai Quoc, Pham Van Dong and Vo Nguyen Giap, at which it was decided to prepare for armed resistance.

In 1941 Nguyen Ai Quoc set foot on Vietnamese soil after an absence of almost 30 years, to head the new and much broader organization that had been set up to lead the resistance struggle, the Vietminh or Vietnam Independence League. Nguyen's plan was to ask the French, whose armed forces were still scattered around the country, to cooperate in resisting the Japanese. The response of the local collaborationist authorities was to cooperate with the Japanese in trying to hunt down the Vietminh. The latter decided to start fighting the Japanese on their own.

In view of the local French attitude, it was agreed that Nguyen should go to Chungking and try to seek Chinese support in the anti-Japanese struggle; at least there seemed a common basis for this. Chiang Kai-shek had transferred his capital to Chungking. Nguyen Ai Quoc's old friend from Canton, Chou En-lai, was also there representing the Communist Eighth Route Army, in the uneasy Kuomintang-Communist coalition that had been patched together again after the Japanese invasion of China. Hoping to throw the agents of his various enemies off the track—including the Japanese now—Nguyen took a new name, Ho Chi Minh. At the first Chinese town after crossing the border, Ho was arrested and flung into jail, fetters on his legs and a yoke around his neck. News of this, when it filtered back, was a terrible blow to Vo Nguyen Giap, Pham Van Dong and the others but they went ahead with the plans that had been agreed on.

The Kuomintang officials knew quite well the identity of Ho Chi Minh, and the leaders in Chungking approved of Vietnamese armed resistance to the Japanese. But they had formed their own organization for this purpose, the *Vietnam Cach Mang Dong Minh Hoi* or Vietnamese Kuomintang, and wanted nothing of the Vietminh except its disappearance. Ho was kept in one prison or another for nearly two years and almost lost his eyesight, only one symptom of a serious deterioration of his fragile health. At one time, he tramped up and down mountain roads for 80 days on end, part of the time with leg chains linked to those that pinioned his elbows behind his back.

When he finally returned to Vietnam, he found that without Kuomintang or French or any other help apart from the organizational line worked out with Giap and Pham Van Dong, large liberated areas had been secured and the ground-work laid for the nationwide armed uprising against the Japanese that was eventually to take place in August 1945.

Taking all that into consideration, plus the long war he subsequently directed against the French, it must be admitted that Ho Chi Minh has had more than his share of revolutionary experience and that for some one who can look back at what was accomplished in over four decades, starting with the struggle and ideas of a single person, there is nothing boastful or exaggerated in contemplating another phase of many more years of struggle.

One of the enormous advantages the Hanoi leaders have over any regime that can be put together in the South is that they are the same team of veterans in revolutionary military-political strategies and tactics who have worked together for almost 40 years. Directly underneath the top leadership is a hard core of cadres who have worked under the same leaders for a quarter of a century. They know each other's minds and thoughts inside out; from below there is absolute confidence in the leadership; from the top there is absolute confidence that policies will be followed and orders strictly executed by the lower-level cadres. They are accustomed to handling new and unexpected situations. They have the confidence of the people—and not only North of the 17th parallel, because the struggle they directed was nationwide. In the South few ever question the devotion of these leaders to the cause of national independence to which they have dedicated their lives. To make any comparison between the experience, caliber and prestige of these men and the attributes of the generals and dollar-seeking politicians that have succeeded each other with such rapidity in the struggle for power in Saigon is superfluous. And it is obviously useless for the Americans to look for a "Ho Chi Minh" in the South; the very fact of American or other western backing would automatically discredit any such "discovery."

A question often asked is how can such men watch the fruits of their life's work being destroyed by American bombers—the factories, bridges, hospitals, schools, institutes, factories, power stations and the rest of it; everything built up since they won the independence struggle either in ruins or likely soon to be. Would it not be better to swallow pride and take advantage of American offers to negotiate? Why is Hanoi, in fact, so unyielding, refusing alike offers of friends to mediate and foes to negotiate? Is Hanoi not taking the "hard" Peking line? Such matters, too, were the object of long off-the-record discussions with Hanoi's leaders. The answers, in résumé, are roughly as follows:

They are furious about the destruction and it will take generations before any Washington administration is forgiven for this. But it is pointed out that the fruits of independence are indestructible, the chief of which is that Vietnamese are masters at least in the northern part of their house. Here a new social-economic regime has been set up; the peasants are masters of their land, the workers of their factories; enormous progress has been made in education and public health. The new social organization in the North has been accepted in the minds and hearts of the people. None of this can be destroyed by bombs— not as long as national independence can be defended, and the leaders are certain that it will be defended in the North and gained in the South.

Negotiations? With the Americans?

The usual answer one gets is that there is nothing for the DRV to negotiate with the Americans. The Americans are committing aggression against the North, they must stop it. If they want to talk about the war in the South, then there must be discussions between belligerents as is normal in any war. In the South, the Americans, their allies and mercenary soldiers of an illegal regime are the belligerents on one side, the National Liberation Front is the belligerent on the other. If the Americans say they want to discuss with us on the basis of the Geneva Agreements, then let them first start implementing the Agreements. Ho Chi Minh, in explaining this to a recent visitor, turned to a map of Vietnam showing American bases studded all over the South. "These bases are knives in the body of Vietnam," he said. "And while they continue to bomb us, they are like someone with a whip in his hands 'inviting' us to sit down and negotiate. We say 'Pull out the knives, throw away your whip and we will negotiate. If we sit down with you with the knives in our body and the whip in your hand, this would be surrender.' And we will never surrender."

It is evident that Hanoi will never negotiate or respond to any moves toward negotiations as long as the American bombings continue; nor will they take advantage of any temporary cessation of the bombings. This would be yielding to force, negotiating under duress, because the logic of a temporary suspension would be that if Hanoi started negotiating but did not accept American terms, the bombings would start again. Therefore they insist on an absolute, unconditional end to the air attacks. Their continuance, or even the threat of resumption in case of a suspension, is taken by the leaders in Hanoi to mean that the Americans do not really want negotiations, but only want to impress the outside world that they do. "On that there is nothing to bargain about," one of the top leaders said. "They are attacking us, they must stop it. We are not attacking the USA, we have nothing to stop."

When they speak of negotiations with the USA, they see this only within the context of a general conference based on the Geneva Agreements. This is made clear in the famous four points of which Hanoi leaders speak whenever negotiations are mentioned. They are as follows:

(1) Recognition of the basic national rights of the Vietnamese people: peace, independence, sovereignty, unity and territorial integrity. According to the Geneva Agreements, the US Government must withdraw from South Vietnam all US troops, military personnel and weapons of all kinds, dismantle all US military bases there, cancel its "military alliance" with South Vietnam. It must end its policy of intervention and aggression in South Vietnam. According to the Geneva Agreements, the US Government must stop its acts of war against North Vietnam, completely cease all encroachments on the territory and sovereignty of the Democratic Republic of Vietnam.

(2) Pending the peaceful reunification of Vietnam, while Vietnam is still temporarily divided into two zones the military provisions of the 1954 Geneva Agreements on Vietnam must be strictly respected: the two zones must refrain from joining any military alliance with foreign countries, there must be no foreign military bases, troops and military personnel in their respective territory.

(3) The internal affairs of South Vietnam must be settled by the South Vietnamese people themselves, in accordance with the program

of the South Vietnam National Liberation Front, without any foreign interference.

(4) The peaceful reunification of Vietnam is to be settled by the Vietnamese people in both zones, without any foreign interference.

"The Government of the DRV," said Pham Van Dong in presenting the four points to the National Assembly on April 13, 1965, "is of the view that the stand expounded above is the basis for the soundest political settlement of the Vietnamese question. If this basis is recognized, favorable conditions will be created for the peaceful settlement of the Vietnamese question and it will be possible to consider the reconvening of an international conference on the pattern of the 1954 Geneva Conference on Vietnam."

The points seem tough at first glance but in fact they are the essence of what was agreed in Geneva in 1954. At the time they were presented, President Johnson, Dean Rusk and others were already talking of a settlement based on the Geneva Agreements. Indeed the American public had gotten the impression by that time that US troops in the South and bombers in the North were at work in defense of the Agreements. The first reaction in Washington was to complain that Hanoi was demanding the withdrawal of US troops, the dismantling of bases, etc., as a "precondition" to any talks.

In fact, Pham Van Dong asked for the recognition of the four points as a "basis" to create "favorable conditions," which was certainly not a demand for withdrawal as a precondition. It was the discovery of this difference by the Mayor of Florence, Sig. La Pira, that led to the resignation of Fanfani as Italian Foreign Minister, the latter while President of the United Nations General Assembly having hurriedly communicated this "discovery" to President Johnson before having informed the Italian government. The fact that this was regarded as such a great "discovery" was due to months of official misinformation from Washington.

In his letter to several heads of state on January 24, 1966, President Ho Chi Minh stated that if the US wished a peaceful solution it should agree to the four-point proposal and prove its intent by "concrete deeds," such as unconditional cessation of the bombing of North Vietnam. As to other "concrete deeds," General Nguyen Van Vinh who, as noted earlier, speaks with considerable authority, wrote in the *Vietnam Courier* (Hanoi, September 23, 1965) regarding withdrawal from the South:

"As for how this withdrawal is carried out, the imperialist camp has lots of experience such as the withdrawal of French troops from Indochina and Algeria, of the American troops from Laos and other parts of the world." In the examples cited, the withdrawals took place after the ceasefire had been negotiated and in accordance with the negotiated terms of the agreement. North Vietnam's leaders regard American intervention in the South and the bombings of the North as violations of the Geneva Agreements which the Americans must halt or promise to halt and provide some concrete evidence that they are sincere in this.

In fact, Washington seems to be scared of the specter of Geneva. The first of Washington's 14 points for peace (January 1966) states rather laconically: "The Geneva Agreements of 1954 and 1962 are an adequate basis for peace in Southeast Asia." What "adequate basis" implies presumably would be defined only at the conference table. (The 1962 Agreement, incidently, was exclusively concerned with Laos.) Point 13 consists of the oft-quoted statement by President Johnson: "The Viet Cong would not have difficulty being represented and having their views represented if for a moment Hanoi decided she wanted to cease aggression. I don't think that would be an insurmountable problem." This sounds remarkably like saying, "after the National Liberation Front has laid down its arms"—especially if taken together with an obviously officially-inspired dispatch from UPI's Washington bureau on December 10, 1965, which said:

"In order to quiet Saigon fears that the United States might 'sell them out' in peace talks, Washington has made it clear to premier Nguyen Cao Ky that it will firmly adhere to two fundamentals:

"(1) In any peace agreement, the National Liberation Front of the Vietcong would be denied any status which could lead to the formation of a coalition government. (2) There could be nothing in any peace treaty which would hinder the South Vietnamese government in its program of total 'pacification' of the countryside. This is considered necessary in order to deny the guerrillas any bases from which to make political inroads or a military comeback.

"The United States has said for some time that it would not negotiate with the National Liberation Front, the political arm of the Vietcong. But at one time officials indicated that some of the non-communist elements fighting with the Vietcong might be considered eligible for participating in the country's political life. This apparently has now been ruled out in the US determination to prevent anything which might serve as the germ of a coalition government."

"So what are we being asked to do?" I heard a top Hanoi official ask a French visitor, after reading him some extracts from the UPI dispatch. "Did General de Gaulle sit down with Hitler and agree on giving him and Laval a free hand to exterminate the *maquis?* Of course he did not. He fought Hitler and later shot Laval. But we are asked to sit down and agree, as the price for saving our skins, to halt any aid to the NLF and concede that a Saigon regime has the right to exterminate them. As no Saigon regime could ever do it alone, we should sit with our arms folded while the Americans tried to do it for them. We should agree that a Laval had the exclusive right to set up a regime in a truncated half of the country. All this we should accept in advance as part of 'unconditional negotiations.' When we do not accept we are accused of being 'belligerent,' of slamming the door to peace. Therefore we must be bombed a bit more until we become 'reasonable.' 'Reasonableness' that means betrayal is not in the vocabulary of any Vietnamese worthy of the name."

To ask an unbeaten military and political machine like the NLF, which claims to control four-fifths of the South Vietnamese countryside and almost two-thirds of the population, to accept any such suicidal arrangements is unthinkable, as it would also be to expect the North to accept anything which is not acceptable to the NLF or is contrary to national interests.

Hanoi is not alone in believing that the only choice being offered by Washington is between unconditional surrender and annihilation. And others also share Hanoi's suspicions that the

US, public statements notwithstanding, intends to occupy at least South Vietnam and to maintain military bases there for the foreseeable future. Thus, at the Vietnam hearings of the Senate Foreign Relations Committee, held between January 28 and February 18, 1966, Senator J. William Fulbright, Chairman of the Committee, in the process of questioning Secretary of State Dean Rusk, made the following comments:

"It is also not clear at all that we are willing to allow any participation of the National Liberation Front either in a provisional government at any time, and, therefore, there is no alternative for them but surrender or annihilation. . . .

"There is the further point about our intention regarding leaving at any time. You have repeated time and again that we are ready to leave. But I think few people in Vietnam, and I believe in other places, can quite understand why we are building such extensive, elaborate, and extremely costly, and very large permanent-type bases, harbors, airfields, military housing, and so on, if we have any intention of leaving in the foreseeable future. In short, I don't think they believe us when we say we will get out. . . .

"Finally, in spite of this statement [of Dean Rusk], the policy seems to be unconditional surrender of the National Liberation Front, or to put it in another way, that this is not a limited war, that we intend to pursue it to victory even though that may result in bringing in the Chinese, and possibly even the Russians, which would force World War Three." (*The Vietnam Hearings*, Vintage, N.Y., 1966; pp. 274–75.)

Under these circumstances, Senator Fulbright told the Secretary of State, the impression is "the only kind of settlement is unconditional surrender. Therefore, there is nothing to negotiate about." In the evasive manner which marked his response to every serious challenge to the war policy, Secretary Rusk asked: "But unconditional surrender of what?" To which Senator Fulbright replied: "That they give up and come to the conference at your mercy and we have total victory. I see no occasion of any disposition to compromise" (p. 277).

On the first day of the hearings, an exchange between Senator Frank Church and Rusk revealed the true worth of Washington's repeated statements that the US has no territorial or permanent military ambitions in South Vietnam. Recalling such statements, and bringing out that in South Korea, 12 years after the truce, there are now approximately 55,000 American combat troops stationed in that country, although Chinese troops were withdrawn immediately after the settlement, Senator Church asked Rusk:

"Does our national interest require and is it our intention to retain a permanent American military base in South Korea?"

To which Rusk replied: "We have no present plans to withdraw our forces from there. This has to be judged on the basis of the total situation in the Far East . . ." (p. 18).

Exchanges such as these show how different is the real face of US policy from the facade presented to the world public in the various "peace offensives" launched from Washington, when subject to critical examination. The evaluation by Senator Fulbright and others of the real value of "unconditional negotiations" differs hardly at all from the evaluations in Hanoi, although the conclusions have been reached by very different processes and from radically opposed viewpoints. As long as this remains US policy, there is not the remotest possibility of even the first moves toward negotiations. "Surrender," like "betrayal," is not in the political vocabulary of Vietnamese revolutionaries.

I have asked if there is not a contradiction between the war aims, as set forth in Hanoi, for liberating the South and reunifying the country and the NLF aims which call for an "independent and neutral" South Vietnam, with unification a matter for some distant future. Points three and four of the Pham Van Dong proposals are referred to, in reply, as stating that Hanoi accepts the Liberation Front program for a "neutral and independent" South Vietnam, incorporated in a neutral zone with Cambodia and Laos. The NLF program also stipulates that reunification shall be a step-by-step affair, with no side imposing its regime on the other.

The NLF position on neutrality and independence, it is stated, can be harmonized with the position of Hanoi's Fatherland Front which provides for a great deal of autonomy in the two parts of Vietnam. Specifically, the latter states:

"Today the social and political situations in the North and South are different. . . . We should take into due consideration the practical situation in both zones, the legitimate interests and aspirations of all sections of the population and at the same time, by negotiations, we should arrive at the holding of free general elections in order to achieve unity, without coercion or annexation of one side by the other. . . . On account of the present situation in both the North and the South, popularly-elected councils and administrative organs with wide powers shall be set up in each locality."

This program was adopted in 1955, long before there was an NLF in the South, but apart from these hints at autonomy, Hanoi has several times stated its approval for the NLF program, including neutrality.

That acceptance of the latter represents a sacrifice as compared to what was promised at Geneva, is noted in the important article by Nguyen Van Vinh, quoted earlier. As the immediate goals of the Liberation Front are "independence, democracy, peace and neutrality," he writes, the Americans ought to accept them. "The Liberation Front demands only a neutral Vietnam. . . . Is it not clear that compared with the Geneva Agreements this is a much lower price which the US imperialists must pay to settle their debts? Is it not clear that this is an honorable way out for them?"

On the question of Vietnamese troop withdrawals from the South, Nguyen Van Vinh wrote: "It would be a sheer illusion if the USA expects to exchange the withdrawal of US and satellite troops from South Vietnam for the withdrawal of the South Vietnam Liberation Army, which they slanderously call 'North Vietnamese troops.' The workers, peasants and other laboring people in South Vietnam who have taken up arms to fight US aggression will go nowhere. They will continue to operate in their fields and native villages. There will be no question of a new regroupment to the North such as carried out in 1954 by the VPA troops operating South of the 17th parallel."

The leaders in Hanoi do not think they are being unreasonable or belligerent in their stand. Apart from surrender in the North and betrayal of the South, they do not see what else they can do, except continue to fight and stick to their terms for settlement. They reject the argument that "might is right" and that because the Americans are very strong and already solidly entrenched in South Vietnam, this must be accepted as a permanent state of affairs. But they admit that they have some difficulties in explaining all this convincingly to well-wishers abroad, whose countries are not faced with similar problems.

When one asks if they are not following the "hard" Peking line, the reply is likely to be unusually heated, lacking the delicacy with which the Vietnamese customarily present their case. The reply, with varying degrees of emphasis according to the personality, runs like this:

"We carried out our own revolution, our own national independence struggle, based on our own needs and conditions. This is a continuation of a millennium-long struggle carried on in our era in the light of Marxist-Leninist scientific thought. We developed our own lines of struggle, directed by our own national leadership. We have never followed any 'line' from outside, nor will we. We are eager to learn from the whole world revolutionary experience, including from the successes and setbacks of fraternal Communist parties. But we must be responsible for our own successes and setbacks.

"Our modern national independence movement started long ago. It was influenced by many factors, including the Sun Yat-sen revolution in China and the October Revolution in Russia. But our struggle had to be different because we were a colony fighting against a foreign occupying power. We had to develop our own line.

"Our present struggle was imposed on us by the Americans, not because of any ideological 'line' from outside. The existence of the socialist camp of which we are now part is a powerful support for us. But whether Peking or Moscow existed or not, whether the socialist camp existed or not, we would have no choice but to take up arms and fight, as our ancestors have always done for natural salvation. We are grateful for Chinese help which they give us willingly and generously. But this does not mean that China tries to impose some 'line' on us or that we would accept it if they did. We have to have a Vietnamese policy dictated by our own national tasks. We accept no advice that runs contrary to our ideas of how we should fulfill that task. We are grateful for Soviet help also but this does not mean that we follow a Moscow 'line' either. We have not fought for over a thousand years to accept some new form of foreign domination now, no matter how it is expressed. Our friends in the fraternal parties understand this quite well and appreciate our position."

As the above summary of an answer makes clear, it is regarded as an unfriendly question, an insult to the Vietnamese revolution, reflecting ignorance of its history, to suggest to any high level cadres that the Hanoi leadership is following any "line" other than a Vietnamese one. The Vietnamese consider their experience gives them every right to have their own line which they do not suggest, however, should be imposed on any other country.

Vietnamese independence is expressed in all sorts of other ways. There are no foreign military bases on her territory nor any foreign troops. There are no Soviet, Chinese, Cuban nor any other foreign pilots flying Vietnamese planes, although thousands of foreign pilots have volunteered for this. There are Soviet radar-controlled anti-aircraft batteries, but the crews are Vietnamese. There are Soviet ground-to-air missiles and a few Soviet specialists to advise on installation and maintenance, but the crews that handle them are Vietnamese. A Vietnamese officer decides if and when and how they are to be fired.

It is not only because this makes application of the second of Pham Van Dong's four points much easier for the DRV than for the Americans, although this is also a factor. There is also the element of national pride. It is the Vietnamese "line" to maintain full control over all their affairs. "The blood shed in this war should be Vietnamese blood," as one leader expressed it to me. "We do not want the other members of the socialist camp to suffer because of our troubles. Let them continue to build socialism in peace, we shall build it in war. Let them give us arms, but the men that handle them will be Vietnamese."

Another important example of their "line" is the attitude to the ideological dispute between Peking and Moscow. "We want unity between the socialist countries," I was told at the highest level. "We consider all socialist countries as our brothers. Nothing can make us change our line on this. All socialist countries are our brothers. This is not opportunism. It is not a policy for today only. This is our long-range stand. Seen from a long-range viewpoint, we consider that the divergencies are temporary family quarrels that should not be shouted about from the rooftops."

Finally, the Vietnamese leaders want to do everything possible to avoid an extension of the conflict. Policy on this was expressed as follows: "US policy is escalation, ours is containment, to try and limit the air war to the North, the ground fighting to the South. If there is any further extension of the war this can come about only by American 'escalation' activities."

All the above represent the most complete answers I could find on the policies and perspectives of the war as seen from North Vietnam during seven weeks I was there.

POSTSCRIPT

Phnom Penh, Cambodia, September 5, 1966.

A few hours before the arrival of President de Gaulle in Cambodia on August 30, 1966, I returned from a fourth visit to the Liberation Front areas of South Vietnam, bringing with me the text of a long interview with the Front's President, Nguyen Huu Tho. Before his historic speech on September 1 at the sports stadium in Phnom Penh, de Gaulle had seen the text of the interview and he was thus the best informed world leader on the latest viewpoint of the NLF leadership.

President de Gaulle had the benefit of a long exchange of views with the Cambodian head of state, Prince Norodom Sihanouk, whose realistic and correct understanding of the war in Vietnam and of how it could be ended has long been known.

De Gaulle's speech was remarkable for many reasons, and not alone because of his forthright statement that the problem can be solved only by the US getting out of Vietnam according to an agreed timetable, leaving Vietnam to solve its own problems. He also demolished the official Washington thesis that "aggression" from the North is the root cause of the war. He placed the responsibility as follows: "The political and military authority of the United States was seen installed in its turn in South Vietnam and, simultaneously, the war gained new strength there in the form of national resistance." In speaking of the "war of national resistance," it should be noted, General de Gaulle used the proper term—one with which he was long familiar as the leader of the French struggle against Hitlerism.

While he doubted that "the American war apparatus will be annihilated on the spot," he found, on the other hand, "no chance that the peoples of Asia will subject themselves to the law of the foreigner who comes from the other shores of the Pacific, whatever his intentions, however powerful his weapons."

His proposed goal of "establishing and guaranteeing the neutrality of the peoples of Indochina and their right to dispose of themselves," as foreseen in the 1954 Geneva Agreements, is acceptable to North Vietnam and the NLF of South Vietnam, as they have made clear many times. His interesting phrase, immediately following, that the political agreement must be reached between "the real powers being exercised there," obviously means the NLF as a belligerent on one side of the conference table and the US and its allies on the other side. It is the stubborn refusal of the US to recognize the NLF as the valid negotiating partner that is the major stumbling block toward even a first step for settlement of the war.

The starting of negotiations, de Gaulle held, "would depend, obviously, on the decision and the commitment which America would have wanted to take beforehand to repatriate its forces within a suitable and determined period of time."

The joint communique of September 2, signed by de Gaulle and Sihanouk, referring to the differences which divide the Vietnamese, states: "It is essentially foreign intervention that, by turning a civil war into an international conflict, has given the hostilities their present dimensions." It goes on to call for a cessation of all military activities in Vietnam "which implies that all foreign powers that have introduced troops here first of all take the commitment to withdraw them within a set period of time and to cease all intervention."

If the US is really looking for a face-saving formula—as has been hinted in Washington from time to time—then seeds for a settlement are there. But the NLF will not settle for only "engagement to disengage." There would have to be very concrete steps toward withdrawal, and there could be no negotiations between South Vietnamese as long as American troops occupied key areas of the country, even if they were not engaged in actual combat.

Further preliminary steps would be necessary after the American engagement to withdraw. The French thinking is that these would include cessation of hostilities in the South and of bombing in the North, and the withdrawal of US troops to their bases. Then there would follow negotiations between the NLF and the Saigon regime. But this, obviously, is unacceptable to the NLF, just as temporary cessation of bombings in the North cannot be accepted as preliminary to negotiations. The obvious threat is that "unless you negotiate my way the bombings will start again and the troops will emerge from the bases again."

The merits of de Gaulle's visit as far as the Vietnam problem is concerned are that the origins of the war were placed in correct perspective and that seeds useful for a settlement were planted. It was the first time that US intervention was so candidly denounced by a leader of the Western world. The visit also permitted direct contact on the spot between NLF representatives and de Gaulle's top advisers.

During my latest visit to the Liberation Front areas of South Vietnam I found NLF President Nguyen Huu Tho confident that the Front could handle whatever troops the US might send into South Vietnam. One reason for this confidence is that the NLF smashed the American dry-season offensive, mainly without committing their regular troops. "The crushing defeat of the strategic counter-offensive of the 1965–66 dry season, for which the Americans very carefully prepared and massed their forces," Nguyen Huu Tho said, "proves their forces are off balance, and are unable to regain the initiative and thus to change the course of the war." He said that 400,000 US troops by the end of this year, and another 100,000 or more next year, could not change the balance of forces since the NLF could reinforce itself more quickly relatively to the US and also since the effectiveness of the Saigon troops falls in proportion as US involvement grows.

"We believe the strength of the army in time of war is a result of many factors," said the NLF President. "Of these, the determining ones are political and moral. We have absolute supremacy over the Americans on the political and moral front. We are also stronger in other fundamental aspects, such as in our strategic position, in our rear areas, in the conduct of the war, and in the grouping of our forces—factors which can decide the outcome on the battlefield."

He repeated that the NLF sees the war as a closely linked military-political struggle, and indicated that conditions are being created for a broad front of national union by alliances between the NLF and other organizations in Saigon and elsewhere. This doubtless would lead to steps in the direction of setting up a coalition government of national union, as envisioned in the

NLF program. Nguyen Huu Tho said that at present there are "great possibilities for extending cooperation with other organizations, forces and personalities that had taken part in the government of Ngo Dinh Diem and other governments that succeeded it." He asserted emphatically that the NLF's stand on neutrality remains unmodified despite massive commitment of US troops and that its program is still based on independence, democracy and peace. The Front, he said, "must have its place and a decisive voice in any political solution."

Regarding prospects for a coalition government of the kind mentioned by Nguyen Huu Tho, it is well to recall that the masses who took part in the Buddhist and student movements in Saigon, Hue, Danang and other cities early in 1966 raised slogans which were in effect identical with those of the Front. The traditional Buddhist leaders isolated themselves from their supporters by rejecting common action with the NLF, and this led important sections of the urban population to turn to support of the Front. New and significant contacts were made with the Buddhist rank and file extending up into the hierarchy, where militant leaders now see that only the NLF can give effective national leadership capable of uniting the country and directing the independence struggle. NLF leaders have told me that the NLF did not "teleguide" the struggle in Saigon, Hue and Danang, but the outcome of the struggle and disillusionment in the wavering compromising attitude of the most publicized Buddhist leaders has turned the rank and file and many urban intellectuals toward the Front and opened up new perspectives for setting up a broadly based government of national coalition.

The NLF insistence on neutrality for an independent South Vietnam is an important rallying point for broad sections of the South Vietnamese people, and its secret supporters reach high up into the ranks of the Saigon administration and army.

In my recent visit to the South, as in the previous ones to the North, all evidence indicates preparations for a very long war, and there seems no doubt that they are capable of fighting indefinitely. But blood continues to be shed in ever greater quantities as escalation continues. A new generation of South Vietnamese has grown up which knows nothing but war. Vietnamese blood and American blood, and the blood of US allies—being shed for what? The Vietnamese, at least, know why. They are defending their homes and soil and will never give up until the foreign aggressors have gone home. In the North they will continue shooting at US planes as long as bombing continues. Armed forces will swoop down from mountain forests to wipe out any troops that try to disembark on their coastlines.

President de Gaulle gave President Johnson valuable advice, when recalling the French experience in getting out of Algeria. He pointed out that far from losing prestige in withdrawing "a distant expedition once it appears unprofitable and unjustified," the United States, on the contrary, would recapture its prestige and audience throughout the world. Beyond doubt the prestige of de Gaulle and of France was vastly enhanced after the withdrawal from Algeria. The same would be true for the United States and President Johnson if they act in time.

INDEX